Japanese
Phrase Book
&
Dictionary

D1354770

Berlitz Publishing
New York   Munich   Singapore

Contacting the Editors
Every effort has been made to provide accurate information in this publication, but changes are inevitable. The publisher cannot be responsible for any resulting loss, inconvenience or injury. We would appreciate it if readers would call our attention to any errors or outdated information. We also welcome your suggestions; if you come across a relevant expression not in our phrase book, please contact us: Berlitz Publishing, 193 Morris Avenue, Springfield, NJ 07081, USA. Email: comments@ berlitzbooks.com

First Printing: December 2007
Printed in Singapore

Publishing Director: Sheryl Olinsky Borg
Editor/Project Manager: Emily Bernath
Senior Editor: Lorraine Sova
Editor: Andrea Pearman
Editorial Assistant: Eric Zuarino
Translation: Nobuo Ogawa
Composition: Datagrafix, Inc.
Cover Design: Claudia Petrilli
Interior Design: Derrick Lim, Juergen Bartz
Production Manager: Elizabeth Gaynor
Cover Photo: © GlowImages/age fotostock
Interior Photos: p. 14 © Studio Fourteen/Brand X Pictures/age fotostock; p. 19 © Brand X Pictures/Punchstock; p. 20 © Pixtal/age fotostock; p. 22 © Corbis/fotosearch.com; p. 36 courtesy of japandriverslicense.com; p. 49 © Purestock/Alamy; p. 55 © 2007 Jupiterimages Corporation; p. 57 © Stockbyte Photography/2002-07 Veer Incorporated; p. 68 © 2007 Jupiterimages Corporation; p. 80 © ImageDJ/Alamy; p. 85 © Netfalls/2003-2007 Shutterstock, Inc.; p. 95 © Angela N. Hunt, 2007 Used under license from Shutterstock, Inc.; p. 99 © BananaStock Ltd.; p. 104 © Daniel Thistlethwaite/PictureQuest; p. 106 © Radu Razvan, 2007 Used under license from Shutterstock, Inc.; p. 109 © 2007 Jupiterimages Corporation; p. 112 © 2007 Jupiterimages Corporation; p. 120 © Fukuoka Irina, 2007 Used under license from Shutterstock, Inc.; p. 129 © Digital Archive Japan/Alamy; p. 137 © Jupiterimages/Brand X/Corbis; p. 139 © Stockbyte/Fotosearch.com; p. 142 © Corbis/2006 Jupiterimages Corporation; p. 144 © David McKee/2003-2007 Shutterstock, Inc.; p. 146, 150, 165 © 2007 Jupiterimages Corporation; inside back cover: © H.W.A.C.

Contents

Survival

Food

People

Fun

Special Needs

Resources

Dictionary

Pronunciation

This section is designed to familiarize you with the sounds of Japanese using our simplified phonetic transcription. The pronunciation of the Japanese sounds is explained below, together with their "imitated" equivalents. This system is used throughout the phrase book. When you see a word spelled phonetically, simply read the pronunciation as if it were English, noting any special rules.

Japanese is a unique language. Apart from a similarity of script (the Japanese adopted Chinese ideograms) it bears no resemblance to Chinese or other Asian languages, except for Korean. Where Japanese comes from is still a matter of conjecture. Japan, its people, customs, and language were almost totally isolated until the late nineteenth century.

Today there are many foreign "loan" words that have been adopted into Japanese. From **pan** (from the Portuguese for bread) to **sportsman**, you will come across many foreign words, the majority of which are from English. At first hearing, you may not recognize such words because of the change in pronunciation and, conversely, you may not be understood when using a "loan" word until you give it a Japanese pronunciation.

Japanese is composed less of vowels and consonants than of syllables, consisting of a consonant and a vowel. Consonants are always followed by vowels, except for **n,** which can occur alone. All syllables are pronounced with equal force: there is no stress except for emphasis.

Consonants

Letter	Approximate Pronunciation	Symbol	Example	Pronunciation
b	approximately as in English	b	バス	basu
ch	approximately as in English	ch	お茶	ocha
d	approximately as in English	d	電車	densha
g	approximately as in English	d	外国	gaikoku
h	approximately as in English	h	箱根	hakone
j	approximately as in English	j	原宿	harajuku
k	approximately as in English	k	観光	kankoo
m	approximately as in English	m	鎌倉	kamakura
p	approximately as in English	p	乾杯	kanpai
s	approximately as in English	s	寿司	sushi
t	approximately as in English	t	成田	narita
f	with lips flattened and without putting lower teeth against lower lip, between an f and an h	f	お風呂	ofuro

Letter	Approximate Pronunciation	Symbol	Example	Pronunciation
n	1. before vowels like n in now	n	長い	nagai
	2. at the end of a word, said without letting your tongue touch the roof of your mouth	n	さん	san
r	with tip of tongue against the gum behind the upper front teeth, between an r and an l	r	りんご	ringo
w [semi-vowel]	the lips are not rounded but left slack	w	分かる	wakaru
z	1. at the beginning of words, like ds in beds	z	ゼロ	zero
	2. In the middle of words like z in zoo	z	水	mizu

Double consonants should be pronounced "long", i.e. hold the sound for a moment. The doubling of a consonant is important as it can change the meaning of a word.

kk		一個		ikko
pp		かっぱ		kappa
tt		ちょっと		chotto

Vowels

Letter	Approximate Pronunciation	Symbol	Example	Pronunciation
a	like the a in father, pronouced forward in the mouth	a	魚	sakana
e	like e in get	e	テレビ	terebi
i	like i in sit	i	イギリス	igirisu
o	like o in note	o	男	otoko
u	like u in put, but without rounding the lips	u	冬	fuyu

Long vowels (aa, ee, ii, oo, uu) are held for twice the amount of time. This is important in Japanese and can change the meaning of words, e.g. **oba(san)** means aunt while **obaa(san)** means grandmother.

Vowel clusters: when two vowels occur together (ie, ai, ue, ao) they should be pronounced separately with each vowel keeping its normal sound.

Consonant/double vowel clusters: (e.g. kya, kyu, kyo) these are two sounds said quickly so that they become one: kya is ki and ya.

Whispered vowels: sometimes i and u are devoiced, that is whispered or even omitted. This happens when i and u occur at the end of a word, or between voiceless consonants: ch, f, h, k, p, s, sh, t, and ts.

Japanese is composed of three different "scripts" or ways of writing: **kanji** (Chinese characters or ideograms), **hiragana** (an alphabet in which each symbol represents a spoken syllable), and **katakana** (another alphabet). These three systems are used in combination to write modern Japanese.

Hiragana is used to link **kanji** characters together. **Katakana** is used to write foreign "loan" words, most of which are English in origin.

In addition to these three "scripts" you will find **romaji**, the Romanized system used to write Japanese. In Japan important signs and names are often given in **romaji**, for example the names of subway stations.

Traditionally Japanese is written from the top to the bottom of the page starting in the upper right-hand corner. Today it is also commonly written horizontally and from left to right. The Japanese phrases you will see in this book incorporate a mixture of **kanji**, **hiragana** and **katakana**, and the pronunciation is in **romaji**. Japanese words and phrases are pronounced very evenly, and stress is used only to emphasize meaning. Pitch does vary however; normal sentences will begin on a high note and finish on a low one.

As in English, questions normally rise in pitch at the end of the sentence.

How to Use This Book

These essential phrases can also be heard on the audio CD.

Sometimes you see two alternatives in italics, separated by a slash. Choose the one that's right for your situation.

Essential

I'm here on *vacation* [*holiday*]/*business*.	観光/仕事で来ました。 *kankoo/shigoto* de kimashita
I'm going to…	…へ行きます。 …e ikimasu
I'm staying at the… Hotel.	…ホテルに泊まっています。 …hoteru ni tomatte imasu

You May See…

税関検査 zeekan kensa	**customs**
免税品 menzeehin	**duty-free goods**
課税 kazee	**goods to declare**

Winter sports

A lift pass for *a day/ five days*, please.	1日/5日分のリフト券、お願いします。 *ichinichi/itsuka* bun no rifutoken onegai shimasu
I want to rent [hire]…	…を借りたいんですが。 …o karitain desu ga
– boots	ースキー靴 sukii gutsu
– a helmet	ーヘルメット herumetto
– poles	ーストック sutokku

Words you may see are shown in *You May See* boxes.

Any of the words or phrases preceded by dashes can be plugged into the sentence above.

Japanese phrases appear in red.

Read the simplified pronunciation as if it were English. For more on pronunciation, see page 7.

Relationships

I'm...   私は … watashi wa ..

When different gender forms apply, the masculine form is followed by ♂; feminine by ♀.

– single   – ひとりです。 hitori

– in a relationship   – 付き合っています。

– married   – 結婚しています。 k

– divorced   – 離婚しました。 rikon shimashita

– separated   – 別居中です。 bekkyo chuu desu

I'm widowed   妻/夫 を亡くしました。 *tsuma♀ / otto♂ o* nakushimashita

▶ For numbers, see page 161.

The arrow indicates a cross reference where you'll find related phrases.

Information boxes contain relevant country, culture and language tips.

 Japan's rail network covers the whole country. There are many different rail operators, but the service is clean, safe, and punctual. First-class cars are called **guriin sha** (green cars) and are marked with a green four-leaf sign.

You May Hear...

英語が少ししかできません。 eego ga sukoshi shika dekimasen

英語はできません。 eego wa dekimasen

Expressions you may hear are shown in *You May Hear* boxes.

I only speak a little English.
I don't speak English.

Color-coded side bars identify each section of the book.

▼ *Survival*

Arrival and Departure

Essential

I'm here on *vacation [holiday]*/*business*.	観光/仕事で来ました。*kankoo/shigoto* de kimashita
I'm going to...	...へ行きます。...e ikimasu
I'm staying at the... Hotel.	...ホテルに泊まっています。...hoteru ni tomatte imasu

You May Hear...

チケット/パスポートをお見せください。*chiketto/pasupooto* o omise kudasai	Your *ticket/passport*, please.
今回の旅行の目的は何ですか。konkai no ryokoo no mokuteki wa nan desu ka	What's the purpose of your visit?
どこにお泊まりですか。doko ni otomari desu ka	Where are you staying?
後、どのくらいいらっしゃいますか。ato donokurai irasshaimasu ka	How long are you staying?
どなたとご一緒ですか。donata to goissho desu ka	Who are you with?

Passport Control and Customs

I'm just passing through.	立ち寄るだけです。tachiyoru dake desu
I would like to declare...	...を申告します。...o shinkoku shimasu
I have nothing to declare.	申告するものはありません。shinkoku suru mono wa arimasen

You May Hear…

申告するものはありますか。 shinkoku suru mono wa arimasu ka	Do you have anything to declare?
関税がかかります kanzee ga kakarimasu	You must pay duty on this.
このバッグを開けてください。 kono baggu o akete kudasai	Please open this bag.

You May See…

税関検査 zeekan kensa	customs
免税品 menzeehin	duty-free goods
課税 kazee	goods to declare
免税 menzee	nothing to declare
入国手続き nyuukoku tetsuzuki	passport control
警察 keesatsu	police

Money and Banking

Essential

Where's…?	…はどこですか。 …wa doko desu ka
– the ATM	– キャッシュコーナー kyasshu koonaa
– the bank	– 銀行 ginkoo
– the currency exchange office	– 両替所 ryoogaejo

What time does the bank *open/close*?	銀行は何時から／までですか。 ginkoo wa nanji *kara/made* desu ka
I'd like to change *dollars/pounds* into yen.	ル/ポンドを円に替えたいんですが *doru/pondo* o en ni kaetain desu ga
I want to cash some traveler's checks [cheques].	トラベラーズチェックを換金したいんですが。 toraberaazu chekku o kankin shitain desu ga

ATM, Bank and Currency Exchange

Can I exchange foreign currency here?	外国通貨の両替はできますか。 gaikoku tsuuka no ryoogae wa dekimasu ka
What's the exchange rate?	為替レートはいくらですか。 kawase reeto wa ikura desu ka
How much is the fee?	手数料はいくらですか。 tesuuryoo wa ikura desu ka
I've lost my traveler's checks [cheques].	トラベラーズチェックをなくしました。 toraberaazu chekku o nakushimashita
My card was lost.	カードをなくしました。 kaado o nakushimashita
My credit cards have been stolen.	クレジットカードを盗まれました。 kurejitto kaado o nusumaremashita
My card doesn't work.	カードが使えません。 kaado ga tsukaemasen

▶ For numbers, see page 161.

You May See...

カードを入れる	insert card
キャンセルする	cancel
消去する	clear
入力する	enter
暗証番号	PIN
引き出す	withdraw funds
当座預金口座から	from checking [current account]
普通預金口座から	from savings
レシート/領収書	receipt

Banks are open from 9 a.m. to 5 p.m. Monday through Friday. Some banks are open on Saturdays and all banks are closed on Sundays, except the bank at Tokyo Airport, which is open 24 hours a day.

Most banks have a foreign currency section. You will need to show your passport to change foreign currency or traveler's checks. You will usually be invited to sit down while the transaction is conducted, which may take as long as 15 minutes. Your name will be called when your money is ready.

You will not be able to use foreign credit cards to get cash from most ATMs, except those run by Citibank (the only foreign bank currently operating in Japan) and the Postal Service. Every post office in Japan has an ATM where you can obtain cash using international credit cards or cash cards from your bank. In rural areas the banks may not have currency exchange facilities. The safest solution is to have cash with you at all times.

You May See...

The monetary system is the yen (円), abbreviated to ¥.
Coins: ¥1, ¥5, ¥10, ¥50, ¥100, and ¥500
Notes: ¥1,000, ¥2,000, ¥5,000, and ¥10,000

Transportation

Essential

How do I get to town?	どうしたら町に行けますか。dooshitara machi ni ikemasu ka
How far is it?	距離はどのくらいですか kyori wa dono kurai desu ka
Where can I buy tickets?	切符はどこで買えますか。kippu wa doko de kaemasu ka

Where's...?	...はどこですか。 ...wa doko desu ka
– the airport	– 空港 kuukoo
– the train [railway] station	– 駅 eki
– the bus station	– バスターミナル basu taaminaru
– the subway [underground] station	– 地下鉄の駅 chikatetsu no eki
A *one-way [single]/ round-trip [return]* ticket.	片道/往復 katamichi/oofuku
How much?	いくらですか。 ikura desuka
Are there any discounts?	割引料金はありますか。 waribiki ryookin wa arimasu ka
Which...?	どちらの... dochira no...
– gate	– ゲート geeto
– line	– 線 sen
– platform	– ホーム hoomu

Where can I get a taxi?	タクシー... doko de n...
Please take me to this address.	この住所ま... onegai shima...
Where can I rent a car?	レンタカーは... wa doko de ka...
Could I have a map?	地図をお願いし...

Is there a discount for...?
– children
– students
– senior ...
– I hav...

Ticketing

When's...to Kyoto?	京都行きの...は何時... ...wa nanji desu ka
– the (first) bus	– (最初の)バス (saisho no) basu
– the (next) flight	– (次の)便 (tsugi no) bin
– the last train	– 終電 shuuden
Where can I buy tickets?	切符はどこで買えますか。kippu wa doko de kaemasu ka
One/Two ticket(s), please.	切符一枚／二枚 お願いします。kippu *ichimai/ nimai* onegai shimasu
For *today/tomorrow*.	今日／あした の *kyoo/ashita* no

▶ For days, see page 166.

▶ For time, see page 164.

A...ticket	...チケット ...chiketto
– one-way [single]	– 片道 katamichi
– round-trip [return]	– 往復 oofuku
– first class	– ファーストクラス faasuto kurasu
– economy class	– エコノミー ekonomii
How much?	いくらですか。ikura desuka

	…はありますか。 …waribiki wa arimasu ka
	– 子供の kodomo no
	– 学生 gakusee
…itizens	– 高齢者 kooreesha
…ve an e-ticket.	Eチケットがあります。 E-chiketto ga arimasu
Can I buy a ticket on the *bus/train*?	バス／電車　の中で切符が買えますか。 *basu/densha* no nakade kippu ga kaemasu ka
I'd like to…my reservation.	予約を…したいんですが。 yoyaku o …shitian desu ga
– cancel	– キャンセル kyanseru
– change	– 変更 henkoo
– confirm	– 確認 kakunin

Plane

Getting to the Airport

How much is a taxi to the airport?	空港までタクシーはいくらですか。 kuukoo made takushii wa ikura desu ka
To…Airport, please.	空港までお願いします。 kuukoo made onegai shimasu

| My airline is… | 航空会社は…です。 kookuu gaisha wa…desu |
| My flight leaves at… | 飛行機の便は…に出ます。 hikooki no bin wa…ni demasu |

▶For time, see page 164.

I'm in a rush.	急いでいます isoide imasu
Can you take an alternate route?	他の道を行ってください。 hoka no michi o itte kudasai
Can you drive *faster/ slower*?	もっと はやく／ゆっくり 運転してくれませんか。 motto *hayaku/yukkuri* unten shite kuremasenka

You May Hear…

どの航空会社をご利用ですか。 dono kookuu gaisha o goriyoo desu ka	What airline are you flying?
国内線ですか，国際線ですか。 kokunaisen desu ka kokusaisen desu ka	Domestic or International?
どのターミナルですか。 dono taaminaru desu ka	What terminal?

You May See…

到着 toochaku	arrivals
出発 shuppatsu	departures
荷物引渡場 nimotsu hikiwatashijo	baggage claim
国内線 kokunaisen	domestic flights
国際線 kokusaisen	international flights
チェックインデスク chekku in desuku	check-in desk
Eチケットチェックイン e-chiketto chekku in	e-ticket check-in
出発ゲート shuppatsu geeto	departure gates

Check-in and Boarding

Where is the check-in desk for flight…?	…便のチェックインデスクはどこですか。 …bin no chekkuin desuku wa doko desu ka
My name is…	…です。…desu
I'm going to…	…へ行きます。…e ikimasu
How much luggage is allowed?	荷物はどれくらい持ち込めますか。nimotsu wa dore kurai mochikomemasu ka
Which gate does flight…leave from?	…便のゲートは何番ですか。? …bin no geeto wa nanban desu ka
I'd like *a window/an aisle* seat.	窓側／通路側 の席をお願いします。*madogawa/ tsuurogawa* no seki o onegaishimasu
When do we *leave/arrive*?	何時に出ますか／着きますか。nanji ni *demasu ka/tsukimasu ka*
Is flight…delayed?	…便は遅れていますか。…bin wa okurete imasu ka
How late will it be?	どのくらい遅れますか。dono kurai okuremasu ka

You May Hear…

次の方 tsugi no kata	Next!
チケット/パスポートをお見せください。*chiketto/ pasupooto* o omise kudasai	Your *ticket/passport*, please.
お荷物はいくつありますか。onimotsu wa ikutsu arimasu ka	How many pieces of luggage do you have?
重量超過です。juuryoo chooka desu	You have excess baggage.
それは手荷物には重すぎます/大きすぎます。sore wa tenimotsu ni wa *omosugimasu/ookisugimasu*	That's too *heavy/ large* for a carry-on [to carry on board].
お荷物は、ご自分で詰められましたか。 onimotsu wa gojibun de tsumeraremashita ka	Did you pack these bags yourself?

誰かに何か運ぶように頼まれましたか。 dareka ni nanika hakobuyooni tanomaremashita ka

ポケットのものを出してください。 poketto no mono o dashite kudasai

靴を脱いでください。 kutsu o nuide kudasai

…便のお客様はご搭乗いただきます。 …bin no okyakusama wa gotoojoo itadakimasu

Did anyone giv[e]
anything to car[ry]
Empty your pock[ets]

Take off your shoes.

Now boarding
flight…

Luggage

Where *is/are* the…?	…はどこですか。 …wa doko desu ka
– luggage carts [trolleys]	– カート kaato
– luggage lockers	– コインロッカー koin rokkaa
– baggage claim	– 荷物引渡場 nimotsu hikiwatashi joo
My luggage has been lost.	荷物がなくなりました。 nimotsu ga nakunarimashita
My luggage has been stolen.	荷物が盗まれました。 nimotsu ga nusumaremashita
My suitcase was damaged.	スーツケースが壊れています。 suutsukeesu ga kowarete imasu

 A Travel Help Line is run by the Japan National Tourist Organization (JNTO). An English-speaking travel expert is available. Ask at your hotel or at a tourist information center for the phone number.

Finding Your Way

Where *is/are* the…?	…はどこですか。 …wa doko desu ka
– currency exchange office	– 両替所 ryoogaejo
– car rental [hire]	– レンタカー rentakaa

Where *is/are* the…?	…はどこですか。…wa doko desu ka
– exit	– 出口 deguchi
– taxis	– タクシー takushii
Is there a…into town?	町に行く…はありますか。machi ni iku …wa arimasu ka
– bus	– バス basu
– train	– 電車 densha
– subway [underground]	– 地下鉄 chikatetsu

▶ For directions, see page 35.

Train

How do I get to the train station?	駅には、どうやって行けますか。eki niwa doo yatte ikemasu ka
How far is it?	距離はどのくらいですか kyori wa dono kurai desu ka
Where *is/are* the…?	…はどこですか。…wa doko desu ka
– ticket office	– きっぷうりば kippu uriba
– information desk	– 案内係 annai gakari
– luggage lockers	– コインロッカー koin rokkaa
– platforms	– ホーム hoomu

▶ For directions, see page 35.

▶ For ticketing, see page 21.

You May See…

ホーム	platforms
案内係	information
予約窓口	reservations

到着

出発

Questions

Could I have a schedule [timetable], please?	時刻表を〈
How long is the trip [journey]?	どのくらいか kakarimasu ka
Do I have to change trains?	乗り換えはあり

Tourists can buy special p
system, as well as on
These passes mu
Japan Air Line
There a
cert

Japan's rail network covers the whole country. There are many different rail operators, and the service is clean, safe, and punctual. First-class cars are called **guriin sha** (green cars) and are marked with a green four-leaf sign. To travel first class you need a special ticket in addition to the normal ticket. Second-class cars have reserved seats and unreserved seats. The former is a little more expensive than the latter.

The types of train are:

新幹線 **shinkansen**, the bullet train. This is the fastest rail service. There are lines in Honshu (main island), Kyushu (south island), and Hokkaido (north island). There are three types: **Nozomi** (the fastest train), **Hikari** and **Kodama**.

特急 **tokkyuu**, limited express. This service is for long-distance travel.

急行 **kyuuko**, the ordinary medium-distance express.

快速 **kaisoku**, rapid train. This commuter service has no surcharge above the basic fare.

普通 **futsuu**, local train. This commuter service has no surcharge above the basic fare.

...sses for unlimited travel on the rail ...buses and ferries, throughout Japan. ...t be bought outside Japan, from offices of ..., travel agents, or Japan Travel Bureau offices.

...e a number of other special discounts for travel along ...ain lines within designated areas over a set period, for example **Shuuyuuken** (周遊券), **Free kippu** (フリーきっぷ), and **Parent-Child Super Pass** (親子スーパーパス). Enquire about these tickets at station travel shops.

Most tickets are bought from vending machines. Find your destination on the diagram above the machines, insert money (change is given), and press the button for the appropriate amount. The station names on the diagram are usually in Japanese only, so it is important to know the characters of the station you are going to.

Departures

Which track [platform] for the train to…?	…行きの列車は何番ホームですか。…iki no ressha wa nan-ban hoomu desu ka
Is this the track [platform] to…?	…行きのホームはここですか。…iki no hoomu wa koko desu ka
Where is track [platform]…?	…行きのホームはここですか。…iki no hoomu wa koko desu ka
Where do I change for…?	…へ行くには、どこで乗り換えますか。…e iku niwa doko de norikaemasu ka

Boarding

Is this seat taken?	この席は空いていますか。kono seki wa aite imasu ka
That's my seat.	そこは私の席です。soko wa watashi no seki desu

You May Hear...

ご乗車の方はお急ぎください。 gojoosha no kata wa oisogi kudasai	**All aboard!**
乗車券を拝見します。 jooshaken o haiken shimasu	**Tickets, please.**
...で乗り換えてください。 ...de norikaete kudasai	**You have to change at...**
次の停車駅は... tsugi no teishaeki wa ...	**Next stop...**

Bus

Where's the bus station?	長距離バスのターミナルはどこですか。 chookyori basu no taaminaru wa doko desu ka
How far is it?	距離はどのくらいですか kyori wa dono kurai desu ka
How do I get to...?	どうしたら...に行けますか。 dooshitara...ni ikemasu ka
Does the bus stop at...?	...に止まりますか。 ...ni tomarimasu ka
Could you tell me when to get off?	下りる場所が来たら、教えてください oriru basho ga kitara oshiete kudasai
Do I have to change buses?	乗り換えはありますか。 norikae wa arimasu ka
Stop here, please!	ここで止めてください。 kokode tomete kudasai

► For ticketing, see page 21.

There are extensive city and rural bus services in Japan. Some towns, such as Hakone, Nagasaki and Kumamoto, have streetcars [trams]. When you board a bus take a numbered ticket and pay at the end. You can save money by buying **kaisuuken**, multiple-ride tickets.

You May See...

バス停留所／バス停   bus stop

入り口／出口   enter/exit

Subway [Underground]

Where's the nearest subway [underground] station?	地下鉄の駅はどこですか。chikatetsu no eki wa doko desu ka
Could I have a map of the subway [underground], please?	地下鉄の路線図をください。chikatetsu no rosenzu o kudasai
Which line for...?	…は、何線ですか。…wa nanisen desu ka
Do I have to transfer [change]?	乗り換えが必要ですか。norikae ga hitsuyoo desu ka
Is this the subway [train] to...?	この電車は…へ行きますか。kono densha wa…e ikimasu
Where are we?	ここは、どこですか。koko wa doko desu ka

▶ For ticketing, see page 21.

Tokyo, Osaka, Nagoya and other big cities have very efficient subway systems. A map showing the various lines and stations is displayed outside **chikatetsu**, subway stations. Trains are frequent and run until around midnight. Station platform signs are in Japanese and English. Avoid rush hours (7-9 a.m. and 5-7 p.m.), when trains can be extremely crowded.

Boat and Ferry

When is the car ferry to Okinawa?	沖縄行きのカーフェリーは、何時ですか。okinawa iki no no kaa ferii wa nanji desu ka

▶ For ticketing, see page 21.

You May See...

救命ボート	life boats
救命ベルト	life jackets

i Ferry services run from Honshu (the main island) to the other islands. Details about ports and sailings may be obtained from the Tourist Information Center (TIC). To sample the charms of the Inland Sea, travel by ferry or hydrofoil is recommended.

Various cruises are available in the Tokyo Bay area, many departing from Hinode Pier (日の出桟橋 **hinode sanbashi**). In Kobe, travelers may enjoy 50-minute port cruises departing from Naka Pier. In Yokohama, you can find 50-minute tours of the harbor leaving from near the retired cruise liner, Hikawa Maru.

Bicycle and Motorcycle

I'd like to rent...	...を借りたいんですが。...o karitain desu ga
– a *3-/10*-speed bicycle	− [３速/10速]の自転車 *sansoku/jussoku* no jitensha
– a moped	− スクーター sukuutaa
– a motorcycle	− オートバイ ootobai
How much per *day/ week*?	[一1日/1週間]、いくらですか。*ichinichi/ isshuukan* ikura desu ka
Can I have a *helmet/ lock*?	ヘルメット／ロックをお願いします。*herumetto/ rokku* o onegai shimasu

Taxi

Where can I get a taxi?	タクシーはどこで乗れますか。takushii wa doko de noremasu ka
I'd like a taxi *now/for tomorrow*.	今 ／ 明日 タクシーをお願いします。*ima/ashita* takushii o onegai shimasu
Pick me up at (*place/time*).	(place)に／(time)に来てください。...ni kite kudasai
I'm going to...	...へ行きます。...e ikimasu
– this address	− この住所 kono juusho
– the airport	− 空港 kuukoo
– the train [railway] station	− 駅 eki
I'm late.	急いでいるんです。isoide irun desu
Can you drive *faster/slower*?	急いで／ゆっくり 運転してください。*isoide/yukkuri* unten shite kudasai
Stop/Wait here.	ここで 止めて／待っていてください。kokode *tomete/matteite* kudasai
How much?	いくらですか。ikura desuka
You said it would cost...yen.	...円ですね。...en desu ne
Keep the change.	お釣りは結構です。otsuri wa kekkoo desu
A receipt, please.	レシートをお願いします。reshiito o onegai shimasu

You May Hear...

どちらまで。dochira made	Where to?
ご住所は。gojuusho wa	What's the address?

Car

Car Rental [Hire]

Where can I rent a car?	レンタカ wa doko
I'd like to rent...	...借りた
– a *2-/4-door* car	– 2/4ドア車 *tsuu/foo* doa sha
– an automatic	– オートマチック ootomachikku
– a car with air conditioning	– エアコン付の車 eakon tsuki no kuruma
– a car seat	– チャイルドシート chairudo shiito
How much...?	いくら ikura
– per *day/week*	– 一日/一週間 ichinichi/isshuukan
– per kilometer	– 一キロ ichi kiro
– for unlimited mileage	– 距離は無制限で kyori wa museigen de
– with insurance	– 保険付きで hoken tsuki de
Are there any special weekend rates?	週末料金はありますか。 shuumatsu ryookin wa arimasu ka

...。 kokusai menkyoshoo	Do you have an international driver's license?
...を見せください。 pasupooto ...asai	Your passport, please.
...お掛けになりますか。hoken o okakeni ...masu ka	Do you want insurance?
...の前金をいただきます。...no maekin o itadakimasu	There is a deposit of...
ここにサインをお願いします。koko ni sain o onegai shimasu	Please sign here.

Gas [Petrol] Station

Where's the gas [petrol] station?	ガソリンスタンドはどこですか。gasorin sutando wa doko desu ka
Fill it up, please.	満タンにしてください。mantan ni shite kudasai
...liters, please.	...リットルお願いします。...rittoru onegai shimasu

▶For numbers, see page 161.

I'll pay *in cash/by credit card*.	現金/（クレジット）カード で払います。 *genkin/(kurejitto) kaado* de haraimasu

You May See...

レギュラー	regular
スーパー	premium [super]
ディーゼル	diesel

34

Asking Directions

Is this the right road to…?	…に行くのは、この道でいいんですか。 …ni ikuno wa kono michi de iin desu ka
How far is it to…?	…まで、どのくらいありますか。 …made dono kurai arimasu ka
Where's…?	…はどこですか。 …wa doko desu ka
– …Street	– …通り …doori
– this address	– この住所 kono juusho
– the highway [motorway]	– 高速道路 koosoku dooro
Can you show me on the map?	この地図で教えてください。 kono chizu de oshiete kudasai
I'm lost.	道に迷いました。 michi ni mayoimashita

You May Hear...

まっすぐ massugu	straight ahead
左 hidari	left
右 migi	right
角/道を曲がったところ *kado/michi* o magatta tokoro	*on/around* the corner
向かい mukai	across
後ろ ushiro	behind
のとなり no tonari	next to
北/南 kita/minami	north/south
東/西 higashi/nishi	east/west
信号 shingoo	traffic light
交差点 koosaten	intersection

You May See...

 stop

 slow down

 minimum speed

 time limited parking

 no standing

 no parking

 dangerous curve

 one way

 no entry

Parking

Can I park here?	ここに駐車してもいいですか。koko ni chuusha shitemo ii desu ka
Where is the nearest parking garage?	この近くに駐車場はありますか。kono chikaku ni chuushajoo wa arimasu ka
How much…?	… いくらですか。… ikura desuka
– per hour	– 1 時間 ichijikan
– per day	– 1 日 ichinichi
– overnight	– 一晩 hitoban

 Street parking is limited. It is common to have your car towed away or booted if you park in illegal spaces. It is an expensive and time-consuming process to get it back. Your hotel may have parking facilities—otherwise the best solution is to use designated parking garages.

Breakdown and Repairs

My car *broke down/won't start*.	車が壊れました。/スタートしません。 kuruma ga *kowaremashita/sutaato shimasen*
Can you fix it?	直してもらえませんか。naoshite moraemasen ka
When will it be ready?	いつ直りますか。itsu naorimasu ka
How much?	いくらですか。ikura desuka

Accidents

There has been an accident.	事故がありました。jiko ga arimashita
Call *an ambulance/the police*.	警察/救急車を呼んでください。*keesatsu/kyuukyuusha* o yonde kudasai

Accommodations

Essential

Can you recommend a hotel in…?	…で良いホテルを教えてください。…de ii hoteru o oshiete kudasai
I have a reservation.	予約してあります。yoyaku shite arimasu
My name is…	…です。…desu
Do you have a room…?	…部屋はありますか。…heya wa arimasu ka
– with a bathroom	– バス付きの basu tsuki no
– with air conditioning	– エアコン付きの eakon tsuki no
Do you have a room for *one/two*?	一人/二人部屋はありますか。*hitori/futari* beya wa arimasuka
For tonight	今晩 konban
For two nights	二晩 futaban
For one week	1 週間 isshuukan

How much?	いくらですか。ikura desuka
Is there anything cheaper?	もっと安い部屋はありますか。motto yasui heya wa arimasu ka
When's check-out?	チェックアウトは何時ですか。chekkuauto wa nanji desu ka
Can I leave this in the safe?	これを金庫に預けたいんですが。kore o kinko ni azuketain desu ga
Can I leave my bags?	荷物を預けたいんですが。nimotsu o azuketain desu ga
Can I have *the bill/a receipt*?	レシート/会計 をお願いします。*kaikee/reshiito* o onegai shimasu
I'll pay *in cash/by credit card*.	現金/（クレジット）カード で払います。*genkin/(kurejitto) kaado* de haraimasu

Finding Lodging

Can you recommend a hotel?	いホテルを教えてください。ii hoteru o oshiete kudasai
What is it near?	どこの近くですか。doko no chikaku desu ka
How do I get there?	どうやって行くんですか。dooyatte ikun desu ka

i

A wide variety of accommodations are available in Japan.

ホテル **hoteru** are Western-style hotels. These are comparable to western hotels.

ビジネスホテル **bijinesu hoteru**, or business hotels, have small rooms, often with no room service. They are clean and comfortable and usually located near train stations.

旅館 **ryokan** are Japanese-style inns. For a taste of the Japanese way of life, a stay at a **ryokan** is recommended. Many are situated in beautiful settings with access to hot springs. Room prices include breakfast, dinner, and service charge. The majority offer only traditional style bathrooms, meals and sleeping arrangements.

Another good way of sampling authentic Japanese lodgings is a 民宿 **minshuku**, or guest house. **Minshuku** are often family run and have an informal, friendly atmosphere. The overnight charge includes dinner and breakfast.

For those with a particular interest in Buddhism, 宿防 **shukuboo**, temple accommodation, will allow you to join in the monks' daily life.

At the Hotel

I have a reservation.	予約してあります。	yoyaku shite arimasu
My name is...	...です。	...desu
Do you have a room...?	...部屋はありますか。	...heya wa arimasu ka
– with a *bathroom [toilet]*/shower	– バス／シャワー付きの	*basu/shawaa* tuki no
– with air conditioning	– エアコンつきの	eakon tsuki no
– that's *smoking/ non-smoking*	– 喫煙／禁煙の	*kitsuen/kinen* no
– for tonight	– 今晩	konban
– for two nights	– 二晩	futaban
– for one week	– 1週間	isshuukan

▶ For numbers, see page 161.

Does the hotel have...?	ホテルに...はありますか。	hoteru ni... wa arimasu ka
– a computer	– コンピュータ	konpyuuta
– an elevator [lift]	– エレベーター	erebeetaa
– (wireless) internet service	– （ワイアレス）インターネットサービス	(waiaresu) intaanetto saabisu
– room service	– ルームサービス	ruumu saabisu
– a gym	– フィットネスセンター	fittonesu sentaa

I need...	...が要るんですが。 ...ga irun desu ga
– an extra bed	– もう一つベッド moo hitotsu beddo
– a cot	– 折り畳みベッド oritatami beddo
– a crib [child's cot]	– ベビーベッド bebii beddo

You May Hear...

パスポート／カード をお願いします。
pasupooto/kaado o onegai shimasu

Your *passport/credit card*, please.

この用紙にご記入ください。 kono
yooshi ni gokinyuu kudasai

Please fill out this form.

ここにサインをお願いします。 koko
ni sain o onegai shimasu

Sign here.

Price

How much per *night/week*?	一泊／一週間いくらですか。 *ippaku/isshuukan* ikura desu ka
Does the price include *breakfast/sales tax [VAT]*?	この料金は朝食／消費税 込みですか。 kono ryookin wa *chooshoku/shoohi zee* komi desu ka

Questions

Where's the...?	...はどこですか。 ...wa doko desu ka
– bar	– バー baa
– bathroom [toilet]	– トイレ toire
– elevator [lift]	– エレベーター erebeetaa
Can I have...?	...をお願いします ...o onegai shimasu
– a blanket	– 毛布 moofu
– an iron	– アイロン airon
– a pillow	– 枕 makura

– soap	– 石鹸 sekken
– toilet paper	– トイレットペーパー toiretto peepaa
– a towel	– タオル taoru
Do you have an adapter for this?	アダプタはありますか。 adaputa wa arimasu ka
How do I turn on the lights?	電気はどうやって付けますか。 denki wa dooyatte tsukemasu ka
Could you wake me at…?	…時に起こしてください。 …ji ni okoshite kudasai
Could I have my things from the safe?	私のものを金庫から出してください。 watashi no mono o kinko kara dashite kudasai
Is/are there any *mail/ messages* for me?	手紙／メッセージがありますか。 *tegami/ messeeji* ga arimasu ka

i

There are two types of toilets that you may find in Japan. Traditional Japanese squat toilets have nothing to sit down on, and the user squats down to use the facility. These toilets flush just like western style. You will also find some toilets like you see in the West. Western style toilets may range from very basic to a high-tech model which will have a heated seat, water jets to wash and warm air to dry, and an automatic mechanism to flush and close the lid.

You May See...

押す／引く	push/pull
トイレ	restroom [toilet]
シャワー	shower
エレベーター	elevator [lift]
階段	stairs

洗濯 室	laundry
起こさないでください	do not disturb
防火扉	fire door
非常口	(emergency) exit
モーニングコール	wake-up call

Problems

There's a problem.	ちょっと困っているんですが。chotto komatte irun desu ga
I've lost my *key/key card*.	鍵／カードキー をなくしました。*kagi/kaado kii* o nakushimashita
I've locked myself out of my room.	鍵を部屋に置いたまま出てきてしまいました。kagi o heya ni oitamama detekite shimaimashita
There's no *hot water/ toilet paper*.	お湯／トイレットペーパーがないんですが。*oyu/toiretto peepaa* ga nain desuga
The room is dirty.	部屋が汚いんですが。heya ga kitanain desu ga
There are bugs in our room.	部屋に虫がいるんですが。heya ni mushi ga irun desuga
The...has broken down.	...が壊れたんですが。...ga kowaretan desuga
Can you fix...?	...を直してもらえますか。...o naoshite moraemasu ka
– the air conditioning	– エアコン eakon
– the fan	– 扇風機 senpuuki
– the heat [heating]	– 暖房 danboo
– the light	– 電気 denki
– the TV	– テレビ terebi
– the toilet	– トイレ toire
I'd like to move to another room.	部屋を替えてください。heya o kaete kudasai

Japan uses the 100 volt electricity system. You may need a converter and/or adapter for your appliances.

Check-out

When's check-out?	チェックアウトは何時ですか。chekkuauto wa nan-ji desu ka
Could I leave my bags here until…?	…まで荷物を置いておいてもいいですか。…made nimotsu o oite oitemo ii desu ka
Can I have *an itemized bill/a receipt*?	明細書/レシート をお願いします。*meesaisho/ reshiito* o onegai shimasu
I think there's a mistake in this bill.	この会計は違っているようですが。kono kaikee wa chigatte iru yoo desu ga
I'll pay *in cash/by credit card*.	現金/（クレジット）カードで払います。*genkin/ (kurejitto) kaado* de haraimasu

 Tipping isn't customary and is officially discouraged. Porters at airports and train stations charge a set fee. Hotels, **ryokan** (Japanese inns) and restaurants add a 10-15% service charge to the bill.

Renting

I've reserved *an apartment/a room*.	アパート/部屋 を借りました。*apaato/heya* o karimashita
My name is…	…です。…desu
Can I have the *key/ key card*?	鍵/カードキー をお願いします。*kagi/kaado kii* o onegai shimasu
Are there…?	…はありますか …wa arimasu ka
– dishes and utensils	– 食器 shokki
– pillows	– 枕 makura

Are there…?	…はありますか …wa arimasu ka
– sheets	– シーツ shiitsu
– towels	– タオル taoru
When/Where do I put out the trash [rubbish]?	ゴミはどこへ/いつ出すんですか。gomi wa *doko e/itsu* dasun desu ka
…is broken.	…が壊れているんですが。…ga kowarete iru n desuga
How does…work?	…はどうやって使えばいいんですか。…wa dooyatte tsukaeba ii n desu ka
– the air conditioner	– エアコン eakon
– the dishwasher	– 皿洗い機 sara arai ki
– the freezer	– 冷凍庫 reetooko
– the heater	– ヒーター hiitaa
– the microwave	– 電子レンジ denshi renji
– the refrigerator	– 冷蔵庫 reezooko
– the stove	– コンロ konro
– the washing machine	– 洗濯機 sentakuki

Household Items

I need…	…が要るんですが。…ga irun desu ga
– an adapter	– アダプタ adaputa
– aluminum [kitchen] foil	– アルミホイル arumi hoiru
– a bottle opener	– 栓抜き sen–nuki
– a broom	– 箒 hooki
– a can opener	– 缶切り kankiri
– cleaning supplies	– クリーニング用品 kuriiningu yoohin
– a corkscrew	– コルクスクリュー koruku sukuryuu

– detergent	– 洗剤 senzai
– dishwashing liquid	– 中性洗剤 tyuusee senzai
– garbage [rubbish] bags	– ごみ袋 gomi bukuro
– a light bulb	– 電球 denkyuu
– matches	– マッチ matchi
– a mop	– モップ moppu
I need...	...が要るんですが。 ...ga irun desu ga
– napkins	– ナプキン napukin
– paper towels	– ペーパータオル peepaa taoru
– plastic wrap [cling film]	– ラップ rappu
– a plunger	– トイレの吸引具 toire no kyuuingu
– scissors	– はさみ hasami
– a vacuum cleaner	– 掃除機 soojiki

▶ For dishes, utensils and kitchen tools, see page 65.

▶ For oven temperatures, see page 169.

Hostel

Do you have any places left for tonight?	今晩、空いている部屋はありますか。 konban aiteiru heya wa arimasuka
Can I have...?	...をお願いします ...o onegai shimasu
– a *single/double* room	– 一人／二人 部屋 *hitori/futari* beya
– a blanket	– 毛布 moofu
– a pillow	– 枕 makura
– sheets	– シーツ shiitsu
– a towel	– タオル taoru
What time do you lock up?	正面玄関は、何時に閉まりますか。 shoomen genkan wa nan-ji ni shimarimasu ka

There are over 500 youth hostels, or ユースホステル **yuusu hosuteru**, located in every part of Japan. They offer the most inexpensive accommodations available. You will often need to share rooms or bathrooms.

Camping

Can I camp here?	ここでキャンプできますか。koko de kyanpu dekimasu ka
Is there a campsite near here?	この近くに、キャンプ場はありますか。kono chikaku ni kyanpu-joo wa arimasu ka
What is the charge per *day/week*?	一日/一週間の料金はいくらですか。*ichi-nichi/isshuukan* no ryookin wa ikura desu ka
Are there...?	…はありますか …wa arimasu ka
– cooking facilities	– 炊事場 suiji-ba
– electrical outlets	– 電源 dengen
– laundry facilities	– 洗濯場 sentakuba
– showers	– シャワー shawaa
– tents for rent [hire]	– 貸しテント kashi tento
Where can I empty the chemical toilet?	ケミカルトイレの汚物を処理したいんですが。kemikaru toire no obutsu o shori shitai n desu ga

You May See...

飲料水	drinking water
キャンプ禁止	no camping
焚火/バーベキュー禁止	no *fires/barbecues*

▶ For household items, see page 44.

▶ For dishes, utensils and kitchen tools, see page 65.

Internet and Communications

Essential

Where's an internet café?	インターネットカフェはどこですか。intaanetto kafe wa doko desu ka
Can I *access the internet/check e-mail*?	インターネット/E メール を使いたいんですが。*intaanetto/iimeeru o tukaitain desu ga*
How much per (half)hour?	一（半）時間いくらですか。ichi(han)jikan ikura desu ka
How do I *connect/ log on*?	接続/ログオン したいんですが。*setsuzoku/ roguon shitain desu ga*
I'd like a phone card, please.	テレホンカードをください。terehon kaado o kudasai
Can I have your phone number?	電話番号を教えてください。denwa bangoo o oshiete kudasai
Here's my *number/ e-mail address*.	これが私の電話番号/E メールアドレス です。kore ga watashi no *denwabangoo/iimeeru adoresu* desu
Call me.	電話してください。denwa shite kudasai
E-mail me.	メールをください。meeru o kudasai
Hello. This is…	もしもし。...ですが。moshi moshi...desu ga
I'd like to speak to…	…さん、お願いします。...san onegai shimasu
Could you repeat that, please?	もう一度、言ってください。moo ichido itte kudasai
I'll call back later.	あとで電話します。ato de denwa shimasu
Bye.	ごめんください。gomen kudasai

| Where's the post office? | 郵便局はどこですか。yuubinkyoku wa doko desu ka |
| I'd like to send this to… | これを …に送りたいんですが。kore o …ni okuri tain desu ga |

Computer, Internet and E–mail ──────

Where's an internet café?	インターネットカフェはどこですか。intaanetto kafe wa doko desu ka
Does it have wireless internet?	ワイアレスインターネットがありますか。waiaresu intaanetto ga arimasu ka
How do I turn the computer *on/off*?	コンピュータを点け/消したいんですが。konpyuuta o *tsuke/keshi* tain desu ga
Can I…?	…ができますか。…ga dekimasu ka
– access the internet	－インターネットアクセス intaanetto akusesu
– check e-mail	－Eメールのチェック iimeeru no chekku
– print	－印刷 insatsu
How much per (half)hour?	一（半）時間いくらですか。ichi(han)jikan ikura desu ka
How do I…?	…はどうしますか。…wa doo shimasu ka
– connect/disconnect	－接続する／接続を切る の *setsuzoku suru/ setsuzoku o kiru* no
– log *on/off*	－ログオン／ログオフ するの *roguon/roguofu* suru no
– type this symbol	－この記号をタイプするの kono kigoo o taipu suru no
What's your e-mail?	Eメールのアドレスは何ですか。iimeeru no adoresuwa nan desu ka
My e-mail is…	私のEメールアドレスは… watashi no iimeeru adoresu wa…

You May See...

閉じる	close
削除する	delete
Eメール	e-mail
ログアウト	exit
ヘルプ	help
インスタント・メッセージ	instant messenger
インターネット	internet
ログイン	login
新着メール	new (message)
オン/オフ	on/off

開ける	open
印刷する	print
保存	save
送信	send
ユーザー名／パスワード	username/password
無線インターネット／ ワイヤレスインターネット	wireless internet

Phone

A *phone card/prepaid phone*, please.	テレホンカード／プリペイド携帯 をお願いします。 terehonkaado/puripeidokeitai o onegai shimasu
How much?	いくらですか。 ikura desuka
My phone doesn't work here.	私の電話が使えません。 watashi no denwa ga tsukaemasen
What's the *area/ country* code for...?	...の 市外局番／国番号 は何番ですか。 ...no shigaikyokuban/kunibangoo wa nanban desu ka
What's the number for Information?	番号案内は何番ですか。 bangoo an-nai wa nanban desu ka
I'd like the number for...	...の番号を教えてください。 ...no bangoo o oshiete kudasai
Can I have your number?	電話番号を教えてください。 denwa bangoo o oshiete kudasai
Here's my number.	これが私の電話番号です。 korega watashi no denwa bangoo desu

▶ For numbers, see page 161.

Call me.	電話してください。 denwa shite kudasai
Text me.	携帯にテキストメールを送ってください。 keitai ni tekisuto meeru o okutte kudasai

I'll call you.	電話します。denwa shimasu
I'll text you.	メールを送ります。meeru o okurimasu

On the Phone

Hello. This is…	もしもし。…ですが。moshi moshi…desu ga
I'd like to speak to…	…さん、お願いします。…san onegai shimasu
Extension…	内…線 naisen…ban
Speak *louder/more slowly*, please.	もう少し 大きい声で／ゆっくり お願いします。mooo sukoshi *ookii koe de/yukkuri* onegai shimasu
Could you repeat that, please?	もう一度、言ってください。moo ichido itte kudasai
I'll call back later.	あとで電話します。atode denwa shimasu
Bye.	ごめんください。gomen kudasai

▶ For business travel, see page 138.

どなたですか。donata desu ka	Who's calling?
少々お待ちください。shoo shoo omachi kudasai	Hold on.
おつなぎします。otsunagi shimasu	I'll put you through.
すみません。今、出ています。sumimasen. ima dete imasu	I'm afraid *he's/she's* not in.
ただ今、電話に出られません。tada ima denwa ni deraremasen	*He/She* can't come to the phone.
ご伝言を承りましょうか。godengon o uketamawarimashoo ka	Would you like to leave a message?
後程／十分後に お電話ください。*nochihodo/ juppungoni* odenwa kudasai	Call back *later/in 10 minutes*.
こちらからお電話いたしましょうか。kochira kara odenwa itashimashoo ka	Can *he/she* call you back?
お電話番号を頂けますか。odenwa bangoo o itadakemasu ka	What's your number?

Fax

Can I *send/receive* a fax here?	ここでファックスを 送れ／受け取れますか。kokode fakkusu o *okure/uketore* masu ka
What's the fax number?	ファックスの番号を頂けますか。fakkusu no bangoo o itadakemasu ka
Please fax this to…	これを …にファックスしてください。kore o…ni fakkusu shite kudasai

You can find public phones in hotel lobbies, on the street and in train stations. You will be able to make overseas phone calls using coins, prepaid telephone cards purchased at a convenience store, or your credit card.

Country codes: Canada and US are 1, UK is 44. Directory assistance in English: 0120-364-463 110 (police) or 119 (fire).

Post Office

Where's the *post office/mailbox [postbox]*?	郵便局／郵便箱 はどこですか。*yuubinkyoku/ yuubinbako* wa doko desu ka
A stamp for this *postcard/letter*, please.	この葉書/手紙用の切手をください。kono *hagaki/tegami* yoo no kitte o kudasai
How much?	いくらですか ikura desuka
I want to send this package by *airmail/ express*	この小包を速達/航空便で送りたいんですが。kono kozutsumi o *sokutatsu/kookuubin* de okuritain desu ga
A receipt, please.	レシートをお願いします。reshiito o onegai shimasu

You May Hear...

税関申告書に記入してください。 zeikan shinkokusho ni kinyuu shite kudasai	Please fill out the customs declaration form.
どのくらいの値段のものですか。dono kurai no nedan no mono desu ka	What's the value?
中には何が入っていますか。naka niwa nani ga haitte imasu ka	What's inside?

53

i Main post offices are open from 8 a.m. to 7 p.m. on weekdays, 9 a.m. to 5 p.m. on Saturdays and 9 a.m. to 12:30 p.m. on Sundays. Local post offices are not open on Sundays and will likely have limited hours during the week. Tokyo International Post Office is open around the clock. Stamps are also sold at hotels and some tobacconists.

Mailboxes, usually red, are found on street corners. You can also mail letters at hotels.

▼ Food

Eating Out

Essential

Can you recommend a good *restaurant/ bar*?	いいレストラン／バー をご存知ですか。 ii *resutoran/baa* o gozonji desu ka
Is there a *traditional Japanese/inexpensive* restaurant nearby?	この近くに料亭/安いレストラン はありますか。 kono chikaku ni *ryootei/yasui resutoran* wa arimasu ka
A table for *one/two*, please.	一人／二人ですが、テーブルがありますか。 *hitori/futari* desu ga, teeburu ga arimasu ka
Could we sit...?	...に座れますか。...ni suwaremasu ka
– here/there	ー ここ／そこ koko/soko
– outside	ー 外 soto
– in a non-smoking area	ー 禁煙席 kin en seki
I'm waiting for someone.	人を待っているんです。hito o matte irun desu
Where's the restroom [toilet]?	トイレはどこですか。toire wa doko desu ka
A menu, please.	メニューをお願いします。menyuu o onegai shimasu
What do you recommend?	何がおいしいですか。nani ga oishii desu ka
I'd like...	...が欲しいんですが ...ga hoshiin desu ga
Some more..., please.	...をお願いします。...o onegai shimasu
Enjoy your meal.	どうぞごゆっくり。doozo goyukkuri
The check [bill], please.	お勘定、お願いします。okanjoo onegai shimasu

Is service included?	サービス料込みですか。 saabisuryoo komi desu ka
Can I pay by credit card?	クレジットカードを使えますか。 kurejitto kaado o tsukaemasu ka
Could I have a receipt, please?	レシートをお願いします。 reshiito o onegai shimasu
Thank you for the food.	ごちそうさまでした。 gochisoo sama deshita

Restaurant Types

Can you recommend...?	...はありますか。 ...wa arimasu ka
– a restaurant	– レストラン resutoran
– a bar	– バー baa
– a cafe	– カフェ kafe
– a fast-food place	– ファストフードの店 fasuto fuudo no mise
– a sushi restaurant	– 寿司屋 sushi ya

Reservations and Questions

I'd like to reserve a table…	…予約をお願いしたいんですが。 yoyaku o onegai shitai n desu ga
– for 2	– 2人です。 futari desu
– for this evening	– 今晩 konban
– for tomorrow at…	– 明日…時に ashita…ji ni
A table for 2.	2人、お願いします。 futari onegai shimasu

▶ For numbers, see page 161.

We have a reservation.	予約してあります。 yoyaku shite arimasu
My name is…	…です。 …desu
Could we sit…?	…に座れますか。 …ni suwaremasu ka
– here/there	– ここ／そこ koko/soko
– outside	– 外 soto
– in a non-smoking area	– 禁煙席 kin enseki
– by the window	– 窓際 madogiwa
Where are the restrooms [toilets]?	トイレはどこですか。 toire wa doko desu ka

You May Hear...

ご予約はいただいておりますでしょうか。 goyoyaku wa itadaite orimasu deshoo ka	Do you have a reservation?
何人様でしょうか。 nannin sama deshoo ka	How many?
喫煙席と禁煙席のどちらがよろしいですか。 kitsuenseki to kin-enseki no dochira ga yoroshii desu ka	Smoking or non-smoking?
ご注文はお決まりですか。 gochuumon wa okimari desu ka	Are you ready to order?

何がよろしいですか。nani ga yoroshii desu ka		What would you like?
…がお薦めです。…ga osusume desu		I recommend…
どうぞごゆっくり。doozo goyukkuri		Enjoy your meal.

Ordering

Waiter!/Waitress!	ちょっとすみません。chotto sumimasen
We're ready to order.	注文したいんですが。chuumon shitain desu ga
May I see the wine list, please?	ワインリストをお願いします。wain risuto o onegai shimasu
I'd like…	…が欲しいんですが …ga hoshiin desu ga
– a bottle of…	– …を一本 …o ippon
– a carafe of…	– …を一カラフ …o hito karafu
– a glass of…	– …一杯 …ippai

▶ For alcoholic and non-alcoholic drinks, see page 79.

The menu, please.	メニューをお願いします。menyuu o onegai shimasu
Do you have…?	…は、ありますか。…wa arimasu ka
– a menu in English	– 英語のメニュー eigo no menyuu
– a fixed–price menu	– セットメニュー setto menyuu
– a children's menu	– 子供用のメニュー kodomo yoo no menyuu
What do you recommend?	何がおいしいですか。nani ga oishii desu ka
What's this?	これは何ですか。kore wan an desu ka
What's in it?	何が入っていますか。nani ga haitte imasu ka
Is it spicy?	これは辛いですか。kore wa karai desu ka
It's to go [take away].	お持ち帰りです。omochi kaeri desu

You May See...

カバーチャージ	cover charge
セット値段	fixed-price
メニュー	menu
本日のメニュー	menu of the day
サービス料金込（別）	service (not) included
スペシャル	specials

Cooking Methods

baked	焼き yaki
boiled	茹で yude
braised	蒸し煮 mushini
breaded	パン粉 panko
creamed	クリームソース kuriimu soosu
diced	さいの目切りの sai no me giri no
filleted	切り身の kiri mi no
fried	揚げ age
grilled	焼き yaki
poached	ポシェ poshe
roasted	ロースト roosuto
sautéed	炒めた itameta
smoked	薫製 kunsei
steamed	蒸し mushi
stewed	煮込み nikomi
stuffed	詰め物 tsumemono

Special Requirements

I am...	私は… watashi wa…
– diabetic	– 糖尿病です toonyoobyoo desu
– lactose intolerant	– 乳糖不対症 nyuutoo futaishoo
– vegetarian	– ベジタリアン bejitarian
I'm allergic to...	…にアレルギーがあります。…ni arerugii ga arimasu
I can't eat...	…は食べられません …wa taberaremasen
– dairy	– 乳製品 nyuuseehin
– gluten	– グルテン guruten
– nuts	– ナッツ nattsu
– pork	– 豚肉 buta niku
– shellfish	– 貝類 kairui
– spicy foods	– 辛い食べ物 karai tabemono
– wheat	– 小麦 komugi
Is it *halal/kosher*?	これは ハラール／コーシャ ですか。 kore wa *haraaru/koosha* desu ka

Dining with Kids

Do you have children's portions?	お子さまメニューはありますか okosama menyuu wa arimasu ka
A highchair, please.	子供のための椅子はありますか。 kodomo no tame no isu wa arimasu ka
Where can I *feed/change* the baby?	どこで 授乳したら／おしめを取り替えたら いいでしょうか。doko de *junyuu shitara/oshime o torikaetara* ii deshoo ka
Can you warm this?	これを暖めてください。kore o atatamete kudaasai

▶ For travel with children, see page 141.

Complaints

How much longer will our food be?	後、どのくらいかかりますか。 ato dono kurai kakarimasu ka
We can't wait any longer.	もう待てません。moo matemasen
We're leaving.	帰ります。kaerimasu
I didn't order this.	注文したのと違います。chuumon shitano to chigaimasu
I ordered…	…を注文しました。…o chuumon shimashita
I can't eat this.	これは、食べられません。kore wa taberaremasen
This is too…	…すぎます …sugimasu
– cold/hot	− 冷/熱 tsumeta/atsu
– salty/spicy	− 塩辛/辛 shio kara/kara
– tough/bland	− 固/味が薄 kata/aji ga usu
This isn't *clean/fresh*.	きれい/新鮮 じゃありません。*kiree/sheinsen* ja arimasen

Paying

The check [bill], please.	お勘定、お願いします。okanjoo onegai shimasu
We'd like to pay separately.	別々に、お願いします。betsubetsu ni onegai shimasu
It's all together.	一緒にお願いします。issho ni onegai shimasu
Is service included?	サービス料込みですか。saabisu ryoo komi desu ka
What's this amount for?	これは何の金額ですか。kore wa nan no kingaku desu ka
I didn't have that. I had…	それは取りませんでした。注文したのは…です。 sore wa torimasen deshita. chuumon shita nowa…desu

Can I pay by credit card?	クレジットカードを使えますか。 kurejitto kaado o tsukaemasu ka
Can I have *an itemized bill/a receipt*?	明細書/レシート をお願いします。 *meesaisho/ reshiito* o onegai shimasu
That was a very good meal.	おいしかった。ごちそうさまでした。 oishikatta. gochisoo sama deshita

Tipping is not a Japanese custom, and there is no need to tip at most restaurants, bars and **izakaya** (taverns). However, some places, especially high-end ones, may include a "service charge" on the bill as gratuity.

Market

Where are the *carts [trolleys]/baskets*?	カート/かごはどこですか。 *kaato/kago* wa doko desu ka
Where is…?	…はどこですか。 …wa doko desu ka

▶ For food items, see page 84.

I'd like some of *that/ those*.	それを少しください。 sore o sukoshi kudasai
Can I taste it?	味見してもいいですか。 ajimi shitemo ii desu ka
I'd like a *kilo/ half-kilo* of …	…が一キロ/五百グラム欲しいんですが …ga *ichikiro/gohyakuguramu* hoshiin desu ga
I'd like…	…が欲しいんですが …ga hoshiin desu ga
– *a liter/half-liter* of…	– …が一リットル/500cc … ga *iti rittoru/ gohyaku shiishii*
– a piece of	– …が一個 …ga ikko
– a slice of	– …が一枚 …ga ichimai
More/Less than that	もう少し 多く/少なく moo sukoshi *ooku/ sukunaku*
How much?	いくら ikura desuka
Where do I pay?	どこで払うんですか。 doko de haraun desu ka

| A bag, please. | 袋をお願いします。 fukuro o onegai shimasu |
| I'm being helped. | 大丈夫です。 daijoobu desu |

▶For conversion tables, see page 168.

You May Hear...

いらっしゃいませ。 irasshaimase	Can I help you?
何がよろしいですか。 naniga yoroshii desu ka	What would you like?
他に何かございますか。 hokani nanika gozaimasu ka	Anything else?
…円でございます。 …en de gozaimasu	That's…yen.

> *i*
> For daily shopping, people usually go to a neighborhood
> fish market, vegetable store, butcher or grocer. Larger
> supermarkets are also popular, as well as food floors of
> department stores (usually located in the basement) where
> you'll find groceries and prepared food. In Tokyo there is a
> famous fish market called **Tsukiji Uoichiba**, which is open
> early in the morning. In Kyoto, **Nishiki Shijo** (Nishiki Market)
> is called the kitchen of Kyoto. Here you can find all kinds of
> local ingredients at more than one hundred stores.

You May See...

賞味期限…	best if used by…
カロリー	calories
無脂肪	fat free
要冷蔵	keep refrigerated
…を極少量含む	may contain traces of…

販売期限		sell by…
菜食主義者向け		suitable for vegetarians

Dishes, Utensils and Kitchen Tools

bottle opener	栓抜き	sennuki
bowl	ボール	booru
can opener	缶切り	kankiri
corkscrew	コルクスクリュー	koruku sukuryuu
cups	カップ	kappu
forks	フォーク	fooku
frying pan	フライパン	furaipan
glasses	グラス/コップ	gurasu/koppu
knife	ナイフ	naifu
measuring *cup/spoon*	計量カップ/スプーン	keeryoo kappu/supuun
napkin	ナプキン	napukin
plates	皿	sara
pot	深鍋	fuka nabe
saucepan	鍋	nabe
spatula	へら	hera
spoon	スプーン	supuun

Meals

i In large Western-style hotels you will have your choice of breakfast: Japanese, English/American or Continental. However, in **ryokan** and **minshuku** (traditional Japanese lodgings) you will be offered only a Japanese-style breakfast. This usually consists of grilled, smoked fish (e.g. salmon), rice, soup and pickles served with tea. While you are out and about, coffee shops provide various dishes for breakfast, including thick slices of buttered toast.

Breakfast

bacon	ベーコン beekon
bread	パン pan
butter	バター bataa
(cold/hot) cereal	(コールド／ホット)シリアル (koorudo/hotto) shiriaru
cheese	チーズ chiizu
coffee/tea	コーヒー/紅茶 koohii/koocha
– with sugar	ー砂糖入りの satoo iri no
– with artificial sweetner	ーダイエットシュガー入りの daietto shugaa iri no
– with milk	ーミルク入りの miruku iri no

I'd like…	…が欲しいんですが …ga hoshiin desu ga
More…please	…をもっとください。…o motto kudasai

– decaf	カフェイン抜きの kafein nuki no
– black	ブラック burakku
cold cuts [charcuterie]	コールドカット koorudo katto
eggs	卵 tamago
a boiled egg	ゆで卵 yude tamago
fried/scrambled eggs	目玉焼き/スクランブルエッグ medama yaki/sukuranburu eggu
fruit juice	フルーツジュース furuutsu juusu
– apple	アップル appuru
– grapefruit	グレープフルーツ gureepufuruutsu
– orange	オレンジ orenji
granola [muesli]	グラノーラ guranoora
honey	蜂蜜 hachimitsu
jam	ジャム jamu
milk	ミルク miruku
muffin	マフィン mafuin
oatmeal	オートミール ooto miiru
omelet	オムレツ omuretsu
rolls	ロールパン rooru pan
sausages	ソーセージ sooseeji
toast	トースト toosuto

With/Without…	…と/…無しで	…to/…nashi de
I can't have…	…は食べられません	…wa taberaremasen

| water | 水 mizu |
| yogurt | ヨーグルト yooguruto |

Appetizers [Starters]

| assorted appetizers | オードブルの盛り
合わせ oodoburu no
moriawase |
| ham | ハム hamu |

| I'd like… | …が欲しいんですが …ga hoshiin desu ga |
| More…please | …をもっとください。 …o motto kudasai |

Japanese snacks	おつまみ otsumami
Japanese pickled vegetables	漬物 tsukemono
olives	オリーブ oriibu
oysters	牡蛎 kaki
salad	サラダ sarada
salami	サラミ sarami

i **Otsumami** are snacks that accompany drinks. You will find such things as salted rice crackers, nuts and dried cuttlefish.

Soup

clear soup	コンソメ konsome
creamed soup	ポタージュスープ potaaju suupu
Japanese clear soup	すまし汁（お吸物） sumashi jiru (osuimono)
miso soup	みそ汁 misoshiru
sweetcorn soup	コーンスープ koon suupu
vegetable soup	野菜スープ yasai suupu
thick soup of chicken, shellfish, prawns, bean curd and vegetables	寄せ鍋 yosenabe
Chinese noodles in broth with meat, fish, seafood or vegetables	ラーメン raamen

With/Without…	…と/…無しで …to/…nashi de
I can't have…	…は食べられません …wa taberaremasen

clear soup made from fish bouillon or seaweed, soy sauce and sake	吸物/すまし汁 suimono/sumashi jiru
wheat noodles in a thick bouillon with fish cake and vegetables	あんかけうどん ankake udon
Chinese noodles in soup with fried vegetables	タンメン tanmen
thinly cut wheat noodles served with cold soup	冷麦 hiyamugi
buckwheat noodles served with cold soup	ざるそば zaru soba
Chinese noodles served with a cold sweet and sour sauce, sliced ham, fish cake and cucumber	冷やし中華 hiyashi chuuka
a winter soup of vegetables, fish cake and eggs	おでん oden

There are two kinds of Japanese soup, which is always part of a traditional meal: **misoshiru**, a light soup often with a few finely chopped pieces of vegetable and bean curd, the distinctive flavor of which comes from the fermented bean paste (miso); and **sumashi jiru** or **suimono**, a clear soup, again with vegetables or bean curd.

In a Japanese meal the soup is not served as a first course, but together with the main course, or with boiled rice and other items.

Egg and Rice Dishes

thick sweet omelet, sometimes used in sushi	卵焼き tamago yaki
fried eggs	目玉焼き medama yaki

I'd like...	...が欲しいんですが ...ga hoshiin desu ga
More...please	...をもっとください。...o motto kudasai

omelet	オムレツ omuretsu
omelet stuffed with fried rice and ketchup	オムライス omuraisu
egg custard with vegetables, fish and chicken	茶碗蒸し chawan mushi
set menu: rice, soup, fish or meat and pickles	定食 teeshoku
fried rice with pork, egg, peas and shrimp	炒飯 chaahan
Japanese-style curry on rice	カレーライス karee raisu

Fish and Seafood

bonito (mackerel family)	鰹 (カツオ) katsuo
cod	鱈 (タラ) tara
cod roe	たらこ tarako
lobster	ロブスター robusutaa
mackerel	鯖 (サバ) saba
mussels	ムール貝 muuru gai
octopus	蛸 (タコ) tako
oysters	牡蠣 (カキ) kaki
salmon	鮭 (サケ) sake
salmon roe	いくら ikura
scallop	帆立貝 hotate gai
squid	いか ika
shrimp [prawns]	海老 (エビ) ebi

With/Without…	…と/…無しで	…to/…nashi de
I can't have…	…は食べられません	…wa taberaremasen

trout	鱒（マス）masu
tuna	鮪（マグロ）maguro
whitebait	白子（シラス）shirasu
raw fish served with soy sauce and horseradish (wasabi)	刺身 sashimi
vinegared rice balls topped with horseradish (wasabi) and raw fish or seafood	寿司 sushi
grilled fish	焼き魚 yaki zakana
fresh fish, seafood and vegetables, coated in batter and deep-fried	天ぷら tenpura
battered fish and vegetables served in a broth with noodles	天ぷらうどん tenpura udon
fish cooked in assorted sauces	煮魚 ni zakana
fish and vegetables cooked in broth	ちり鍋 chirinabe

Fish and seafood play a major role in Japanese cuisine. This is reflected in the variety and quality of available seafood. Typical ways of eating fish include broiled, boiled, deep fried and raw. Prepared raw fish (**sushi** or **sashimi**) is dipped into a mixture of soy sauce and **wasabi** (horseradish paste), and enjoyed with steaming hot rice. **Sashimi** is usually served as part of a larger meal, and **sashimi** restaurants are often expensive. You can also buy **sushi** at the food court of a department store, at a supermarket, or at a take-out restaurant.

I'd like…	…が欲しいんですが …ga hoshiin desu ga
More…please	…をもっとください。…o motto kudasai

Meat and Poultry

bacon	ベーコン beekon
beef	牛肉 gyuu niku
chicken	鶏肉/チキン tori niku/chikin
duck	鴨 kamo
filet steak	ひれステーキ hire suteeki
ham	ハム hamu
lamb	ラム肉 ramu niku
liver	レバー rebaa
pork	豚肉 buta niku
sausages	ソーセージ sooseeji
steak	ステーキ suteeki
sirloin steak	サーロインステーキ saaroin suteeki
thin slices	薄切り usugiri
thin slices of beef with vegetables, bean curd and thin noodles cooked in sauce	すき焼 sukiyaki
thinly sliced beef cooked with vegetables in broth	しゃぶしゃぶ shabu shabu
Korean dish of marinated meat and vegetables grilled on a hot plate at the table	焼肉 yaki niku
breaded pork cutlet fried and served with shredded cabbage and rice	とんかつ tonkatsu

With/Without…	…と/…無しで …to/…nashi de
I can't have…	…は食べられません …wa taberaremasen

| deep fried breaded pork on bed of rice cooked with egg, onions and peas | カツ丼 katsudon |
| barbequed chicken pieces marinated in sweet soy sauce | 焼き鳥 yakitori |

rare	レア rea
medium	ミディアム midiamu
well-done	ウェルダン werudan

Noodles

buckwheat noodles served with shredded meat or egg with vegetables and broth—may be served hot or cold	そば soba
wheat-flour noodles served with shredded meat or egg with vegetables and broth—may be served hot or cold	うどん udon
Chinese noodles in a broth served hot or cold	ラーメン raamen
very thin wheat-flour noodles, usually served chilled	そうめん soomen

Noodle dishes are very popular, and make delicious and filling meals. It's not considered bad manners to make slurping noises while eating your noodles—the extra oxygen is supposed to improve the taste.

| I'd like… | …が欲しいんですが …ga hoshiin desu ga |
| More…please | …をもっとください。…o motto kudasai |

Vegetables

cabbage	キャベツ kyabetsu
carrot	にんじん ninjin
Chinese cabbage	白菜 hakusai
cucumber	きゅうり kyuuri
eggplant [aubergine]	なす nasu
gingko nut	ぎんなん ginnan
green bean	さやいんげん saya ingen
leek	ねぎ negi
lettuce	レタス retasu
mushroom	マッシュルーム masshuruumu
onion	玉ねぎ tamanegi
pea	グリンピース gurinpiisu
potato (in Western dishes)	ポテト poteto
potato (in Japanese dishes)	じゃがいも jagaimo
pumpkin	かぼちゃ kabocha
tomato	トマト tomato
white radish	大根 daikon
shitake mushroom	椎茸（しいたけ） shiitake
enokidake mushroom	なめたけ nametake
stir-fried vegetables	野菜炒め yasai itame

With/Without…	…と/…無しで …to/…nashi de
I can't have…	…は食べられません …wa taberaremasen

stewed vegetables	野菜の煮物 yasai no nimono
Japanese pickled vegetables	漬物 tsukemono
boiled green vegetables with soy sauce	おひたし ohitashi

 Salad isn't part of traditional Japanese cuisine; pickled vegetables are a more authentic equivalent. However, many Western-style restaurants and bars offer a variety of salads and dressings.

Spices and Staples

beans	豆 mame
bread	パン pan
buckwheat noodles	そば soba
Chinese noodles in soup	ラーメン raamen
MSG (monosodium glutamate)	味の素 aji no moto
pasta	パスタ pasuta
paste made from fermented soybeans	味噌 miso
black pepper	コショウ/胡椒 koshoo
rice	ご飯 gohan
salt	塩 shio
spaghetti	スパゲッティ supagetti
soy (sauce)	醤油 shooyu
wheat noodles	うどん udon

I'd like…	…が欲しいんですが …ga hoshiin desu ga
More…please	…をもっとください。 …o motto kudasai

> In a Japanese meal, rice is served separately in an individual
> bowl. It is short grained and slightly sticky. Although plain, rice
> is perhaps the most important part of the meal. The Japanese
> consider it a heresy to mix other food items or sauces into the
> rice. It is customary to raise the bowl to your lips and push the
> rice into your mouth with chopsticks. On a Western-style menu
> rice is usually called **raisu**.

Fruit

apple	りんご ringo
banana	バナナ banana
cherry	さくらんぼ sakuranbo
grapefruit	グレープフルーツ gureepufuruutsu
grape	ぶどう budoo
melon	メロン meron
orange	オレンジ orenji
peach	桃 momo
pear	梨 nashi
persimmon	柿 kaki
strawberry	苺（いちご）ichigo
tangerine	蜜柑（みかん）mikan
watermelon	西瓜（すいか）suika

With/Without…	…と/…無しで	…to/…nashi de
I can't have…	…は食べられません	…wa taberaremasen

Dessert is not a typical part of a Japanese meal. Called **dezaato**, it was introduced from the West. Today you will find a variety of Western-style desserts along with a number of desserts made from more typical Japanese ingredients.

Dessert

rice cake, traditionally eaten at New Year	餅 mochi
gelatin cubes made from seaweed, with sweet bean paste and fruit	あんみつ anmitsu
sweet bean paste covered with shaved ice and sweet syrup	氷あずき koori azuki
gelatin cubes made from seaweed, topped with fruit and syrup	フルーツみつ豆 furuutsu mitsumame
crème caramel	プリン purin
ice cream	アイスクリーム aisu kuriimu
hot steamed bun with sweet azuki bean paste	あんまん anman
chocolate parfait	チョコレートパフェ chokoreeto pafe
arrowroot cake with molasses syrup	葛餅 kuzu mochi
sweet pancake with butter and syrup	ホットケーキ hotto keeki
fruit salad	フルーツサラダ furuutsu sarada
balls of rice covered with bean paste	おはぎ ohagi
sweet red bean paste soup	お汁粉 oshiruko

I'd like...	...が欲しいんですが ...ga hoshiin desu ga
More...please	...をもっとください。...o motto kudasai

Drinks

Essential

May I see the *wine list/drink menu*?	ワインリスト／ドリンクメニュー を見せてください。 *wain risuto/dorinku menyuu* o misete kudasai
What do you recommend?	何がおいしいですか。nani ga oishii desu ka
I'd like a *bottle/glass* of *red/white* wine.	赤／白 ワイン を一本／一杯お願いします。*aka/shiro* wain o *ippon/ippai* onegai shimasu
The house wine, please.	ハウスワインをお願いします。hausu wain o onegai shimasu
Another *bottle/glass*, please.	もう一本／一杯お願いします。moo *ippon/ippai* onegai shimasu
I'd like a local beer.	地ビールをお願いします。jibiiru o onegai shimasu
Can I buy you a drink?	一杯おごらせてください。ippai ogorasete kudasai
Cheers!	乾杯！kanpai
A *coffee/tea*, please.	コーヒー／紅茶をお願いします。*koohii/koocha* o onegai shimasu
black	ブラック burakku
With...	…と ...to
– milk	ー ミルク miruku
– sugar	ー 砂糖 satoo
– artificial sweetener	ー ダイエットシュガー daietto shugaa

With/Without...	…と／…無しで ...to/...nashi de
I can't have...	…は食べられません ...wa taberaremasen

I'd like…	…をお願いします。 …o onegai shimasu
– juice	フルーツジュース furuutsu juusu
– soda	炭酸飲料 tansan inryoo
– (sparkling/still) water	ソーダ水／水 soda sui/mizu
Is the tap water safe to drink?	水道水は飲んでも安全ですか。 suidoosui wa nondemo anzen desu ka

Non-alcoholic Drinks

coffee	コーヒー koohii
– black	ブラック burakku
– with milk	ミルク入りの miruku irino
– with sugar	砂糖入りの satoo iri no
– with artificial sweetner	ダイエットシュガー 入りの daietto shugaa iri no

iced coffee	アイスコーヒー aisu koohii
hot chocolate	ココア kokoa
juice	ジュース juusu
apple juice	アップルジュース appuru juusu
orange juice	オレンジジュース orenji juusu
lemonade	レモネード remoneedo
milk (when ordering at a restaurant)	ミルク miruku
milkshake	ミルクセーキ mirukuseeki
tea	紅茶 koocha
green tea	お茶 ocha
iced tea	アイスティー aisu tii
water	水 mizu
mineral water	ミネラルウォーター mineraru wootaa
soda water	ソーダ sooda
tonic water	トニック tonikku

Sake is the general name for any drink, traditional or imported, but is usually used to refer to rice wine, more properly known as **nihonshu**.

Japanese green tea is often served in restaurants free of charge. It is drunk without any additions.

A special tea, **matcha** is used for traditional ceremonies. It was first used by Buddhist monks to help them stay awake while meditating. Its spiritual roots are still apparent today in the highly ritualized tea ceremony. The tea should not only refresh you physically, but also give you time to appreciate the beauty of the objects used in the ceremony and the surroundings, all leading to meditative reflection. You may find tea-ceremony rooms in museums and gardens, where you'll be able to try a little **matcha** for a small fee.

You May Hear...

何か飲みますか。nani ka nomimasu ka	Can I get you a drink?
ミルク/砂糖 を入れますか。miruku/satoo o iremasu ka	With *milk/sugar*?
炭酸水ですか，非炭酸水ですか。tansansui desu ka hi tansansui desu ka	Carbonated or non-carbonated [still] water?

Aperitifs, Cocktails and Liqueurs

single/double	シングル/ダブル shinguru/daburu
straight [neat]/on the rocks	ストレート/オンザロック sutoreeto/onzarokku
a glass/a bottle	グラス1杯/瓶1本 gurasu ippai/bin ippon
brandy	ブランデー burandee
gin	ジン jin
gin and tonic	ジントニック jin tonikku
plum wine	梅酒 umeshu
rum	ラム酒 ramu shu
sherry/vermouth	シェリー/ベルモット sherii/berumotto
shoochuu (*see below*)	焼酎 shoochuu
vodka	ウォッカ wokka

whisky	ウイスキー uisukii
with water	水割り mizuwari
with soda water	ウイスキーソーダ uisukii sooda

Beer

bottled	瓶入り bin iri
draft [draught]	生 nama
dark beer	黒ビール kuro biiru

The Japanese produce a number of different beers which are similar to English and German lager beers. Three well known-brands are Asahi®, Kirin® and Sapporo®. In most bars you can choose between bottled and draft.

Shoochuu is a distilled liquor (up to 90 proof) made from either sweet potatoes or rice. This drink is not commonly known to visitors to Japan and is held in rather low esteem by some Japanese. The best **shoochuu** is, however, excellent and is comparable to tequila, vodka, and other such spirits. Whisky is now a very popular drink in Japan and there are a number of good Japanese brands—the best known is probably Suntory®.

Wine

red wine	赤ワイン aka wain
white wine	白ワイン shiro wain
blush [rosé] wine	ロゼ roze
dry/sweet/sparkling	ドライ/スイート/スパークリング dorai/suiito/supaakuringu
chilled/at room temperature	冷えた/室温の khieta/shitsuon no

sake/nihonshu	お酒/日本酒 osake/nihonshu
– cold	– 冷 hiya
– lukewarm	– 人肌 hitohada
– hot	– 熱燗 atsukan

 Grape wine isn't an authentic Japanese drink and until recently was not produced in Japan. You will not find wine widely available outside of Western-style restaurants, big hotels, and department stores. Even there you may find the choice limited to sweeter white wines, although this is changing.

Rice wine, known as **nihonshu** but usually referred to as **sake**, is the traditional Japanese wine. The snacks traditionally served with sake are known as **otsumami**. These include seafood and meat served on skewers, sweet-salty dried cuttlefish, sashimi and more.

This drink is served at table in small china carafes and is drunk from small cups or wooden boxes. You can ask for your **nihonshu** to be served cold, warm or hot.

Menu Reader

almond	アーモンド aamondo
aperitif	食前酒 shokuzenshu
apple	りんご ringo
apple juice	アップルジュース appuru juusu
apricot	アンズ anzu

artichoke	アーティチョーク aatichooku
artificial sweetner	ダイエットシュ ガー daietto shugaa
asparagus	アスパラバス asuparagasu
avocado	アボカド abokado
bacon	ベーコン beekon
banana	バナナ banana
bass	バス basu
bay leaf	ベイリーフ bei riifu
bean	豆 mame
bean sprout	もやし moyashi
beef	牛肉 gyuu niku

beer	ビール biiru
beet	ビート biito
black pepper	胡椒 koshoo
blush [rosé] wine	ロゼ roze
bonito (mackerel family)	鰹 (カツオ) katsuo
brandy	ブランデー burandee
bread	パン pan
breast (chicken)	胸肉 muneniku
broth	コンソメ konsome
buckwheat noodles	そば soba
butter	バター bataa
cabbage	キャベツ kyabetsu
carrot	にんじん ninjin
cauliflower	カリフラワー karifurawaa
celery	セロリ serori
cheese	チーズ chiizu
cherry	さくらんぼ sakuranbo
chicken	鶏肉 *tori niku*
chickpea	ひよこ豆 hiyoko mame
Chinese cabbage	白菜 hakusai
Chinese meat dumplings	餃子 gyooza
Chinese noodles in soup	ラーメン raamen
chocolate	チョコレート chokoreeto
cod	鱈 (タラ) tara
cod roe	たらこ tarako
coffee	コーヒー koohii

cookie [biscuit]	クッキー kukkii
cornmeal	コーンミール koon miiru
crab	蟹 kani
cracker	クラッカー kurakkaa
cream	生クリーム nama kuriimu
cucumber	きゅうり kyuuri
curried	カレー karee
custard	カスタード kasutaado
deep-fried	揚げ age
dried squid	するめ surume
duck	鴨 kamo
dumpling	餃子 gyooza
eel	鰻 unagi
egg	卵 tamago
eggplant [aubergine]	なす nasu
endive	エンダイブ endaibu
escarole	キクヂシャ kikujisha
fig	いちじく ichijiku
fish	魚 sakana
fish cake	蒲鉾 kamaboko
French fries [chips]	ポテトフライ poteto furai
fruit	フルーツ/果物 furuutsu/kudamono
fruit salad	フルーツサラダ furuutsu sarada
garlic	ニンニク ninniku

gin	ジン jin
ginger	生姜 shooga
gingko nuts	ぎんなん ginnan
granola [muesli]	グラノーラ guranoora
grapefruit	グレープフルーツ gureepufuruutsu
grape	ぶどう/葡萄 budoo
green bean	さやいんげん saya ingen
green tea	お茶 ocha
grilled tofu	焼き豆腐 yaki doofu
guava	グアバ guaba
ham	ハム hamu
hamburger	ハンバーガー hanbaagaa
hazlenut	ヘーゼルナッツ heezeru nattsu
heart	心臓 shinzoo
herb	ハーブ haabu
herring	ニシン nishin
honey	蜂蜜（ハニー）hachimitsu (hanii)
hot chocolate	ココア kokoa
hot dog	ホットドッグ hotto doggu
ice (cube)	氷 koori
ice cream	アイスクリーム aisu kuriimu
iced coffee	アイスコーヒー aisu koohii

iced tea	アイスティー aisu tii
jam	ジャム jamu
Japanese pickled vegetables	漬物 tsukemono
Japanese snacks	おつまみ otsumami
Japanese-style curry on rice	カレーライス karee raisu
juice	ジュース juusu
ketchup	ケチャップ kechappu
kiwi	キウィ kiui
lamb	ラム肉 ramu niku
leek	ねぎ/葱 negi
leg	もも肉 momo niku
lemon	レモン remon
lemonade	レモネード remoneedo
lentil	平豆 hiramame
lettuce	レタス retasu
lime	ライム raimu
liver	レバー rebaa
lobster	ロブスター robusutaa
mackerel	鯖（サバ）saba
mango	マンゴー mangoo
margerine	マーガリン maagarin
mayonnaise	マヨネーズ mayoneezu
meat	肉 niku
melon	メロン meron
milk (a carton)	牛乳 gyuunyuu
milk (when ordering in a restaurant)	ミルク miruku

milkshake	ミルクセーキ mirukuseeki
mineral water	ミネラルウォーター mineraru wootaa
mint	ミント minto
miso (paste made from fermented soybeans)	味噌 miso
miso soup	みそ汁 misoshiru
MSG (monosodium glutamate)	味の素 aji no moto
mushrooms	マッシュルーム masshuruumu
mussels	ムール貝 muuru gai
mustard	からし karashi
mutton	マトン maton
noodle	うどん udon
nougat	ヌガー nugaa
nuts	ナッツ nattsu
oatmeal	オートミール ooto miiru
octopus	蛸（タコ）tako
olive	オリーブ oriibu
olive oil	オリーブオイル oriibu oiru
omelet	オムレツ omuretsu
onion	玉ねぎ tamanegi
orange	オレンジ orenji
orange juice	オレンジジュース orenji juusu
oregano	オレガノ oregano
ox	オックス okkusu

oxtail	オックステール okkusu teeru
oyster	牡蛎 kaki
pancake	パンケーキ pankeeki
papaya	パパイヤ papaiya
paprika	パプリカ papurika
pasta	パスタ pasuta
pastry	ペストリー pesutorii
peach	桃 momo
peanut	ピーナッツ piinattsu
pear (Japanese pears are round and hard like apples)	梨 nashi
pea	グリンピース gurinpiisu
pecan	ピーカン piikan
pepper (vegetable)	ピーマン pepper
persimmon	柿 kaki
pickle [gherkin]	ピクルス pikurusu
pineapple	パイナップル painappuru
pizza	ピザ piza
plum	プラム puramu
pork	豚肉 buta niku
potato—when in Japanese dishes	馬鈴薯/じゃがいも bareesho/jagaimo
potato—when in Western-style dishes	ポテト poteto
potato chpis [crisps]	ポテトチップ poteto chippu
prune	プルーン puruun
pudding	プリン purin

pumpkin	かぼちゃ kabocha
quail	ウズラ uzura
rabbit	ウサギ肉 usagi niku
radish	ラディッシュ radisshu
raisin	レーズン reezun
relish	レリッシュ rerisshu
rice	ご飯 gohan
rice crackers	煎餅 senbee
roast	ロースト roosuto
roast beef	ローストビーフ roosuto biifu
roll	ロールパン rooru pan
rum	ラム酒 ramu shu
salad	サラダ sarada
salami	サラミ sarami
salmon	鮭（サケ）sake
salmon roe	いくら ikura
salt	塩 shio
sandwich	サンドイッチ sandoitchi
sardine	イワシ iwashi
sauce	ソース soosu
sausage	ソーセージ sooseeji
savory pancakes	お好み焼き okonomiyaki
scallion [spring onion]	ねぎ negi
scallop	帆立貝 hotate gai
scotch	スコッチ sukotchi
seafood	魚介類/海鮮料理 gyokai rui/kaisen ryoori

seaweed (dried in flat sheets)	海苔 nori
sherry	シェリー sherii
shitake mushroom	椎茸（しいたけ） shiitake
shrimp [prawns]	海老 ebi
soda	炭酸飲料 tansan inryoo
soda water	ソーダ sooda
soup	スープ suupu
soy (sauce)	醤油 shooyu
spaghetti	スパゲッティ supagetti
spinach	ほうれん草 hoorensoo
squash	かぼちゃ kabocha
squid	いか ika
steak	ステーキ suteeki
strawberry	苺（いちご） ichigo
sugar	砂糖 satoo
sweets	甘いもの amaimono
sweet potato	サツマイモ satsumaimo
swordfish	メカジキ mekajiki
syrup	シロップ shiroppu
tangerine	蜜柑（みかん） mikan
tarragon	タラゴン taragon
tea (black)	紅茶 koocha
toast	トースト toosuto
thyme	タイム taimu
tofu (soybean curd)	豆腐 toofu
tomato	トマト tomato

tonic water	トニック tonikku
tripe	胃袋 ibukuro
trout	鱒（マス）masu
truffles	トリュフ toryufu
tuna	鮪（マグロ）maguro
turkey	七面鳥 shichimenchoo
turnip	かぶ kabu
vanilla	バニラ banira
veal	子牛の肉 koushi no niku
vegetable	野菜 yasai
venison	鹿の肉 shika no niku
vermouth	ベルモット berumotto
vodka	ウォッカ wokka
vinegar	酢 su
water	水 mizu
watercress	クレソン kureson
watermelon	西瓜（すいか）suika
wheat	小麦 komugi
wheat noodles	うどん udon
whisky	ウイスキー uisukii
white radish	大根 daikon
whitebait	白子（シラス）shirasu
wild boar	猪 inoshishi
wine	ワイン wain
yogurt	ヨーグルト yooguruto
zucchini [courgette]	ズッキーニ zukkiini

▼ *People*

Talking

Essential

Hello.	こんにちは konnichiwa
How are you?	お元気ですか。ogenki desu ka
Fine, thanks.	はい、おかげさまで。hai okage sama de
Excuse me! (to get attention)	失礼します。shitsuree shimasu
Do you speak English?	英語ができますか。eego ga dekimasu ka
What's your name?	お名前は。onamae wa
My name is…	…です。…desu
Pleased to meet you.	よろしくお願いします。yoroshiku onegai shimasu
Where are you from?	どちらからですか。dochira kara desu ka
I'm from the *U.S./U.K.*	アメリカ／イギリス からです。*amerika/igirisu* kara desu
What do you do?	何をしていますか。nani o shite imasu ka
I work for…	…に勤めています。…ni tsutomete imasu
I'm a student.	学生です。gakusee desu
I'm retired.	退職しました。taishoku shimashita
Do you like…?	…は好きですか。…wa suki desu ka
Goodbye.	さようなら。sayoonara
See you later.	それではまた。sore dewa mata

It is customary in Japan to address people by their last name first, though more recently when meeting foreigners many Japanese will give their surname last. Generally, the suffix **-san** (Mr., Mrs., or Ms.) is used after the last name, so someone with a last name of Honda and a first name of Kenji would be addressed as Honda-san. Never use **san** to talk about yourself.

Communication Difficulties

Do you speak English?	英語ができますか eego ga dekimasu ka
Does anyone here speak English?	英語ができる人はいますか。eego ga dekiru hito wa imasu ka
I don't speak (much) Japanese.	(あまり)日本語ができません。(amari) nihongo ga dekimasen
Could you speak more slowly?	ゆっくり言ってくれませんか。yukkuri itte kuremasen ka
Could you repeat that?	もう一度、言ってくれませんか。moo ichido itte kuremasen ka
Excuse me? [Pardon?]	すみません sumimasen
What was that?	何ですか。nan desu ka
Please write it down.	書いてください。kaite kudasai
Can you translate this for me?	訳してください。yakushite kudasai
What does *this/that* mean?	これ/それは、何という意味ですか。*kore/sore* wa nan to yuu imi desu ka
I understand.	分かりました。wakarimashita
I don't understand.	分かりません。wakarimasen
Do you understand?	分かりますか。wakarimasu ka

You May Hear...

英語が少ししかできません。	eego ga sukoshi shika dekimasen	I only speak a little English.
英語はできません。	eego wa dekimasen	I don't speak English.

Making Friends

Hello.	こんにちは	konnichi wa
Pleased to meet you!	初めまして。	hajimemashite
Good morning.	おはようございます。	ohayoo gozaimasu
Good afternoon.	こんにちは。	konnichi wa
Good evening.	こんばんは。	konban wa
My name is...	...です。	...desu
What's your name?	お名前は。	onamae wa
I'd like to introduce you to...	...さんをご紹介します	...san o goshookai shimasu
Nice to meet you.	よろしくお願いします。	yoroshiku onegai shimasu
How are you?	お元気ですか。	ogenki desu ka
Fine, thanks.	はい、おかげさまで。	hai, okage sama de.
And you?	いかがですか。	ikaga desu ka

Japanese has three levels of speech: plain, polite and honorific. Which level to use is determined by how well you know the other person, and also by age, social status and situation. Female speakers tend to employ polite speech, and young people often use plain speech. Japanese culture emphasizes respect, so honorific speech is appropriate when a younger person addresses an older person, or a person in an organization or company addresses a superior. Honorific speech is also used when trying to sell goods or services to others.

An appropriate greeting for the first meeting between adults is **Hajimemashite**, which literally means *For the first time*. In subsequent meetings, this changes to **konnichi wa** (during the day) or **konban wa** (in the afternoon), which are still polite. **Yaa** (for men) and **Ara** (for women), both meaning *Hi!* are only appropriate among friends, in a casual setting.

In this book, you will find polite or honorific speech style, depending on the situation.

Travel Talk

I'm here…	…で来ました。…dekimashita
– on business	– 仕事 shigoto
– on vacation [holiday]	– 観光[休暇] kankoo
– studying	– 研究 kenkyuu
I'm staying for…	…間、滞在しています。…kan taizai shiteimasu
I've been here…	…間前に、来ました。…kan mae ni kimashita
– a day	– 日 nichi/hi
– a week	– 週 shuu
– a month	– 月 tsuki

▶ For numbers, see page 161.

Where are you from?	どちらからですか。dochira kara desu ka
I'm from…	…から来ました。…kara kimashita

Relationships

Who are you with?	どなたとご一緒ですか。donata to goissho desu ka
I'm on my own.	一人です。hitori desu
I'm with my…	…と一緒です。…to issho desu
– husband/wife	– 主人/家内 shujin/kanai
– boyfriend/girlfriend	– ボーイフレンド/ガールフレンド booifurendo/gaarufurendo
– friend(s)	– 友人 yuujin
– colleague(s)	– 同僚 dooryoo
When's your birthday?	誕生日はいつですか。tanjoobi wa itsu desu ka
How old are you?	何歳ですか。nansai desu ka
I'm…	…歳です。…sai desu

▶ For numbers, see page 161.

Are you married?	結婚していますか。kekkon shite imasu ka
I'm...	私は... watashi wa ...
– single	– ひとりです。hitori desu
– in a relationship	– 付き合っています。tsukiatte imasu
– married	– 結婚しています。kekkon shite imasu
– divorced	– 離婚しました。rikon shimashita
– separated	– 別居中です。bekkyo chuu desu
I'm widowed.	妻/夫 を亡くしました。 *tsuma♀ / otto♂* o nakushimashita
Do you have *children/grandchildren*?	お子さん／お孫さん がいますか。 *okosan/ omagosan* ga imasu ka

Work and School

What do you do?	(お仕事は) 何をしていますか。(oshigoto wa) nani o shite imasu ka
What are you studying?	何を勉強していますか。nani o benkyoo shite imasu ka
I'm studying...	...を勉強しています。...o benkyoo shite imasu
I work *full time/part time*.	フルタイム／パートタイム です。 *furu/paato* taimu desu
I'm between jobs.	求職中です。kyuushoku chuu desu
I work at home.	自宅で仕事をしています。jitaku de shigoto o shiteimasu
Who do you work for?	どちらにお勤めですか。dochira ni otsutome desu ka
I work for...	...に勤めています。...ni tsutomete imasu
Here's my business card.	名刺をどうぞ。meeshi o doozo

▶ For business travel, see page 138.

Weather

What's the weather forecast for tomorrow?	明日の予報は何ですか。 *ashita no yohoo wa nan desu ka*
What *beautiful/terrible* weather!	なんて きれいな／いやな 天気なんでしょう。 *nante kireina/iyana tenki nan deshoo*
It's *cool/warm*.	涼しい／暖かい です。 *suzushii/atatakai desu*
It's *rainy/sunny*.	雨／晴れ です。 *ame/hare desu*
It's *snowy/icy*.	雪が降って／凍って います。 *yuki ga futte/ kootte imasu*
Do I need *a jacket/an umbrella*?	上着／傘 がいりますか。 *uwagi/kasa ga irimasu ka*

▶For temperature, see page 169.

Romance

Essential

Would you like to go out for a *drink/meal*?	飲み物／食事 いかがですか。 *nomimono/shokuji ikaga desu ka*
What are your plans for *tonight/tomorrow*?	今晩／明日 予定はありますか。 *konban/ashita yotee wa arimasu ka*
Can I have your number?	電話番号を教えてくれませんか。 *denwa bangoo o oshiete kuremasen ka*
Can I join you?	ご一緒してもいいですか。 *goissho shitemo ii desu ka*
Can I buy you a drink?	一杯おごらせてください。 *ippai ogorasete kudasai*
I like you.	あなたが気に入りました。 *anata ga kini irimashita*
I love you.	あなたが好きです。 *anata ga suki desu*

Making Plans

Would you like to…?	…行きませんか。…ikimasen ka
– go out for coffee	– コーヒーを飲みに koohii o nomi ni
– go for a drink	– 飲みに nomi ni
– go out for a meal	– 食事に shokuji ni
What are your plans for…?	…予定はありますか。…yotee wa arimasu ka
– tonight	– 今晩 konban
– tomorrow	– 明日 ashita
– this weekend	– 今週末 konshuumatsu
Where would you like to go?	どこに行きましょうか。doko ni ikimashoo ka
I'd like to go to…	…に行きたいです。…ni ikitai desu
Do you like…?	…は好きですか。…wa suki desu ka
Can I have your *number/e-mail*?	電話番号／Eメールアドレスを 教えてくれませんか。*denwabangoo/iimeeru adoresu* o oshiete kuremasen ka

▶ For e-mail and phone, see page 47.

Pick-up [Chat-up] Lines

Can I join you?	ご一緒してもいいですか。goissho shitemo ii desu ka
You're very attractive.	あなたはとても魅力的ですね。anata wa totemo miryokuteki desu ne
Let's go somewhere quieter.	もっと静かなところへ行きましょう。motto shizukana tokoro e ikimasshoo

Accepting and Rejecting

I'd love to.	喜んで yorokonde
Where should we meet?	どこで待ち合わせましょうか。 doko de machiawasemashoo ka
I'll meet you at *the bar/your hotel*.	バー／ホテル で会いましょう。 *baa/hoteru* de aimashoo
I'll come by at…	…に来ます。 …ni kimasu
What's your address?	住所は？ juusho wa
Thank you, but I'm busy.	申し訳ありませんが、約束があります。 mooshiwake arimasen ga yakusoku ga arimasu
I'm not interested.	興味がありません。 kyuoomi ga arimasen
Leave me alone.	構わないでください。 kamawanaide kudasai
Stop bothering me!	邪魔するのはやめてください。 jama suru nowa yamete kudasai

Getting Physical

Can I *hug/kiss* you?	抱き締めても／キスしてもいいですか。 *dakishimetemo/kisushitemo* ii desu ka
Yes.	はい hai
No.	いいえ iie
Stop!	やめて！ yamete

Sexual Preferences

Are you gay?	あなたはゲイですか。anata wa gee desu ka
I'm...	私は ...です。watashi wa ...desu
– heterosexual	– ヘテロ hetero
– homosexual	– ホモ homo
– bisexual	– バイ bai
Do you like *men/ women*?	男性／女性 が好きですか。*dansei/josei* ga suki desu ka

▶ For informal and formal "you," see page 159.

▼ Fun

Sightseeing

Essential

Where's the tourist information office?	観光案内所はどこですか。 kankoo annaijo wa doko desu ka
What are the main points of interest?	観光名所はどこですか。 kankoo meesho wa doko desu ka
Do you have tours in English?	英語のツアーがありますか。 eego no tsuaa ga arimasu ka
Could I have a *map/guide* please?	地図／案内書 をください。 *chizu/annaisho* o kudasai

The Japan National Tourist Organization (JNTO) operates Tourist Information Centers (TIC) in Japan and overseas. These centers provide a wealth of information, including free maps, brochures, tour itineraries and advice on travel to and within Japan. They will give advice on the "goodwill guide", a free guide service, as well as professional guide services.

In Tokyo, at Tokyo and Shinjuku rail stations, you will find special centers called Information for Foreigners (**gaikokujin annai jo**) providing foreigners with information on sightseeing, travel, living in Tokyo and much more.

Tourist Information Office

Can you recommend...?	...はありますか。 ...wa arimasu ka
– a boat trip	– 遊覧船 yuuransen
– an excursion	– 遊覧旅行 yuuran ryokoo
– a sightseeing tour	– 観光ツアー kankoo tsuaa

| Do you have any information on…? | …の案内はありますか。…no annai wa arimasu ka |

Tours

I'd like to go on the tour to…	…へのツアーに参加したいんですが。…e no tsuaa ni sanka shitain desu ga
When's the next tour?	次のツアーはいつですか。tsugi no tsuaa wa itsu desu ka
Are there tours in English?	英語のツアーがありますか。eego no tsuaa ga arimasu ka
Is there an English-speaking *guide/audio guide*?	英語のガイド／オーディオがありますか。eego no *gaido/oodio* ga arimasu ka
What time do we *leave/return*?	何時に 出ますか／戻りますか。nanji ni *demasu ka/modorimasu ka*
We'd like to have a look at the…	…を見たいんですが。…o mitain desu ga
Can we stop here…?	…ここで止まれますか。…koko de tomaremasu ka
– to take photographs	－写真を撮りたいんですが、shashin o toritain desu ga
– to buy souvenirs	－お土産を買いたいんですが、omiyage o kaitain desu ga
– to use the bathrooms [toilets]	－トイレに行きたいんですが、toire ni ikitain desu ga
Is there access for the disabled?	身体障害者は入れますか。shintai shogaisha wa hairemasu ka

▶ For ticketing, see page 21.

Sights

Where is the...?	...はどこですか。 ...wa doko desu ka
– art gallery	– 美術館 bijutsukan
– battle site	– 戦場跡 senjoo ato
– botanical garden	– 植物園 shokubutsuen
– Buddhist temple	– お寺 otera
– castle	– お城 oshiro
– castle remains	– 城跡 shiro ato
– cemetery	– 墓地 bochi
– church	– 教会 kyookai
– downtown area	– 繁華街 hankagai
– fountain	– 噴水 funsui
– historic site	– 史跡 shiseki
– (war) memorial	– (戦争) 記念碑 (sensoo) kinen hi
– museum	– 博物館 hakubutsukan
– five-story [storey] pagoda	– 五重塔 gojuu no too
– Imperial palace	– 皇居 kookyo

Where is the…?	…はどこですか。 …wa doko desu ka
– park	– 公園 kooen
– parliament building	– 国会議事堂 kokkai gijidoo
– Shinto shrine	– 神社 jinja
– shopping area	– 商店街 shootengai
– statue	– 銅像 doozoo
– theater [theatre]	– 劇場 gekijoo
– town hall	– 市役所 shiyakusho
Can you show me on the map?	この地図で教えてください。 kono chizu de oshiete kudasai

▶ For directions, see page 35.

Impressions

It's…	…ですね。 …desu ne
– amazing	– すごい sugoi
– beautiful	– 美しい utsukushii
– boring	– つまらない tsumaranai
– interesting	– おもしろい omoshiroi
– magnificent	– 立派 rippa
– romantic	– ロマンチック romanchikku
– strange	– 変 hen
– superb	– 素晴らしい subarashii
– terrible	– ひどい hidoi
– ugly	– 醜い minikui
I like it./I don't like it.	好きです/好きではありません。 suki *desu/dewa arimasen*

Religion

Where's...?	...はどこですか。 ...wa doko desu ka
– the cathedral	– 大聖堂 daiseedoo
– the *Catholic/ Protestant* church	– カトリック/プロテスタント教会 *katorikku/ purotesutanto* kyookai
– the mosque	– 回教寺院 kaikyoo jiin
– the Shinto shrine	– 神社 jinja
– the synagogue	– ユダヤ教会堂 yudaya kyookaidoo
– the *Buddhist/Zen* temple	– 寺/禅寺 tera/zendera
What time is *mass/ the service*?	ミサ/礼拝 は何時ですか。 *misa/reehai* wa nanji desu ka

Shopping

Essential

Where is the shopping center?	ショッピングセンターはどこですか。 shoppinngu sentaa wa doko desu ka
I'm just looking.	ちょっと見ているだけです chotto miteiru dake desu
Can you help me?	ちょっと，お願いします。 chotto onegai shimasu
I'm being helped.	大丈夫です。 daijoobu desu
How much?	いくらですか。 ikura desu ka
That one.	それ sore
That's all, thanks.	それで結構です。 sorede kekkoo desu
Where can I pay?	どこで払うんですか。 doko de haraun desu ka

I'll pay *in cash/by credit card*.	現金/（クレジット）カードで払います。 *genkin/(kurejitto) kaado de haraimasu*
A receipt, please.	レシートをお願いします。 reshiito o onegai shimasu

i Japanese usually shop at department stores for clothing and household items. You will not be able to bargain at department stores, which tend to sell more expensive items. There are two large, upscale shopping centers, Roppongi Hills and Omote Sando Hills, in Tokyo. If you want to find bargain items, visit a flea market at the neighborhood temple or town square, where vendors sell used kimonos, household items or antiques. If you are interested in small electronic items such as audio-video equipment, home appliances, computers, computer games or anime and anime related characters, visit Akihabara in Tokyo. Several blocks surrounding the Akihabara Station are filled with stores selling all kinds of items.

Stores

Where's the...?	...はどこですか。 ...wa doko desu ka
– antiques store	– 骨董品店 kottoohinten
– bakery	– パン屋 pan ya
– bank	– 銀行 ginkoo
– bookstore	– 本屋 hon ya
– clothing store	– 洋服屋 yoofukuya
– delicatessen	– デリカテッセン derikatessen
– department store	– デパート depaato
– health food store	– 健康食品店 kenkoo shokuhin ten
– jeweler	– 宝石店 hooseki ten
– liquor store [off-licence]	– 酒屋 sakaya
– market	– マーケット maaketto
– pastry shop	– ケーキ屋 keekiya
– pharmacy [chemist]	– 薬局 yakkyoku
– produce [grocery] store	– 食料品店 shokuryoohin ten
– shoe store	– 靴屋 kutsuya
– shopping mall [shopping centre]	– ショッピングセンター shoppinngu sentaa
– the souvenir store	– お土産屋 omiyageya
– the supermarket	– スーパー suupaa
– the tobacconist	– タバコ屋 tabakoya
– the toy store	– おもちゃ屋 omochaya

Services

Can you recommend...?	いい...はありますか。ii...wa arimasu ka
– a barber	– 床屋 tokoya
– a dry cleaner	– ドライクリーニング店 dorai kuriiningu ten
– a hairdresser	– 美容院 biyooin
– a laundromat [launderette]	– コインランドリー koin randorii
– a nail salon	– ネイルサロン neeru saron
– a spa	– スパ supa
– a travel agency	– 旅行代理店 ryokoo dairiten
Can you...this?	...できますか。...dekimasu ka
– alter	– 仕立て直し shitatenaoshi
– clean	– 洗濯 sentaku
– mend	– 修繕 shuuzen
– press	– プレス puresu
When will it be ready?	いつできますか。itsu dekimasu ka

Spa

I'd like...	...をお願いしたいんですが。 ...o onegai shitain desuga
– an *eyebrow/bikini* wax	– まつげ／ビキニ ワックス *matsuge/bikini wakkusu*
– a facial	– フェーシャル feesharu
– a manicure/pedicure	– マニキュア／ペディキュア manikyua/ pedikyua
– a (sports) massage	– マッサージ massaaji

Do you do…?	…をしますか。 …o shimasu ka
– acupuncture	– 鍼 hari
– aromatherapy	– アロマセラピー aromaserapii
– oxygen treatment	– 酸素治療 sanso chiryoo
Is there a sauna?	サウナがありますか。 sauna ga arimasu ka

For relaxation in a traditional setting, visit one of many hot springs throughout Japan. You will find special facilities at hotels and Japanese inns near hot spring areas. A hot spring is enjoyed just like a bath: traditionally no bathing suit is worn, and there are separate areas for men and women. Sometimes you will find a smaller area for family use. In addition to the hot springs, there are many day spas in the cities, and hotel and resort spas are also available. Prices are comparable to the west, but tipping is not expected.

Hair Salon

I'd like…	…をお願いしたいんですが。 …o onegai shitain desu ga
– an appointment for *today/tomorrow*	– 今日／明日の予約 *kyoo/ashita* no yoyaku
– some color	– カラー karaa
– some highlights	– ハイライト hairaito
– my hair styled	– スタイル sutairu
– a haircut	– カット katto
I'd like a trim.	そろえてもらいたいんですが。 soroete moraitain desu ga
Don't cut it too short.	切りすぎないでください。 kiri suginai de kudasai
Shorter here.	ここをもう少し短くして下さい。 koko o moo sukoshi mijikaku shite kudasai

Sales Help

What are the opening hours?	開店時間は何時ですか。 kaiten jikan wa nanji desu ka
Where *is/are*...?	...はどこですか。 ...wa doko desu ka
– the cashier [cash desk]	– 会計 kaikee
– the escalator	– エスカレーター esukareetaa
– the elevator [lift]	– エレベーター erebeetaa
– the fitting room	– 試着室 shichakushitsu
– the store directory [guide]	– 店内の案内 tennai no annai
Can you help me?	ちょっと，お願いします。 chotto onegai shimasu
I'm just looking.	ちょっと見ているだけです。 chotto miteiru dake desu
I'm being helped.	大丈夫です。 daijoobu desu
Do you have...?	...は、ありますか。 ...wa arimasu ka
Could you show me...?	...を見せてください。 ...o misete kudasai
Can you *ship/wrap* it?	届けて／包装して ください。 *todokete/hoosoo shite* kudasai
How much?	いくらですか。 ikura desu ka
That's all, thanks.	それで全部です。 sore de zenbu desu

▶ For clothing items, see page 122.

▶ For food items, see page 84.

▶ For souvenirs, see page 119.

You May Hear...

いらっしゃいませ。irasshaimase	Can I help you?
少々お待ちください。shooshoo omachi kudasai	One moment.
何がよろしいですか。nani ga yoroshii desu ka	What would you like?
他に何かございますか。hoka ni nanika gozaimasu ka	Anything else?

Preferences

I'd like something...	…のが欲しいんですが。...no ga hoshiin desu ga
– cheap/expensive	– 安い/高い yasui/takai
– larger/smaller	– もっと大きい/小さい motto *ookii/chiisai*
– from this region	– この地方から kono chihoo kara
Is it real?	本物ですか。honmono desu ka
Could you show me *this/that*?	これ／それ を見せてください。*kore/sore* o misete kudasai

Decisions

That's not quite what I want.	私が思っているのと少し違うんですが。watashi ga omotte iru noto sukoshi chigaun desu ga
No, I don't like it.	あまり好きではありません。amari suki dewa arimasen
That's too expensive.	高すぎます。taka sugimasu
I'd like to think about it.	考えさせてください。kangae sasete kudasai
I'll take it.	それにします。sore ni shimasu

Bargaining

That's too much.	高すぎます。 taka sugimasu
I'll give you…	…でどうですか。 …de doo desu ka
I only have…yen.	…円しかありません。 …en shika arimasen
Is that your best price?	もっと安くなりませんか。 motto yasuku narimasen ka
Can you give me a discount?	割引してくれませんか。 waribiki shite kuremasen ka

▶ For numbers, see page 161.

Paying

How much?	いくらですか。 ikura desu ka
I'll pay…	…で払います。 …de haraimasu
– in cash	− 現金 genkin
– by credit card	− （クレジット）カード (kurejitto) kaado
– by traveler's check [cheque]	− トラベラーズチェック toraberaazu chekku
A receipt, please.	レシートをお願いします。 reshiito o onegai shimasu

Visitors to Japan can use the international credit cards at most stores, however, withdrawing cash using your credit card is limited to a small number of ATMs.

You May Hear...

お支払いはどうなさいますか。oshiharai wa doo nasaimasu ka	How are you paying?
このカードで承認が得られませんでした。 kono kaado de shoonin ga eraremasen deshita	This transaction has not been approved.
他に身分証明はお持ちですか hoka ni mibun shoomeisho wa omochi desu ka	May I have additional identification?
現金でお願いします。genkin de onegai shimasu	Cash only, please.
小銭はございますか。kozeni wa gozaimasu ka	Do you have any smaller change?

Complaints

I'd like...	...ですが ... desu ga
– to exchange this	– 交換したいん kookan shitain
– to return this	– 返品したいん henpin shitain
– a refund	– 返金してもらいたいん henkin shite moraitain
– to see the manager	– マネージャーに会いたいん maneejaa ni aitain

Souvenirs

dolls	人形 ningyoo
electrical goods	電気製品 denki seehin
fans	扇子 sensu
cloth wrap traditionally used as a handbag	風呂敷 furoshiki
handcrafts	工芸品 koogeehin
kimono	着物 kimono

lacquerware	漆器 shikki
ornaments	装飾品 sooshokuhin
paper crafts	紙細工 kami zaiku
pearls	真珠 shinju
porcelain	磁器 jiki
pottery	焼き物 yakimono
prints	版画 hanga
sake (rice wine)	日本酒 nihonshu
woodblock prints	木版 mokuhan
yukata (cotton bathrobe)	浴衣 yukata
Can I see *this/that*?	これ／それ をお願いします。*kore/sore* o onegai shimasu
It's the one in the *window/display case*.	ショーウィンドー／ケース にあるのです。*shoouindoo/keesu* ni aru no desu
I'd like...	...が欲しいんですが ...ga hoshiin desu ga
– a battery	－ 電池 denchi

– a bracelet	– ブレスレット buresuretto
– a brooch	– ブローチ buroochi
– earrings	– イヤリング iyaringu
– a necklace	– ネックレス nekkuresu
– a ring	– 指輪/リング *yubiwa/ringu*
– a watch	– 腕時計 ude dokee
I'd like…	…が欲しいんですが …ga hoshiin desu ga
– copper	– 銅 doo
– crystal (quartz)	– 水晶 suishoo
– diamonds	– ダイアモンド daiamondo
– *white/yellow* gold	– プラチナ/金 *purachina/kin*
– pearls	– 真珠 shinju
– pewter	– ピューター pyuutaa
– platinum	– プラチナ purachina
– sterling silver	– 純銀 jungin
Is this real?	本物ですか。 honmono desu ka
Can you engrave it?	…を彫り込んでください。 …o horikonde kudasai

You will have no difficulty finding any number of souvenirs and presents to take home. There is something for everybody and in every price range. If you are buying electrical goods, remember that Japan uses 100 volts and that television/video systems may not be compatible.

Different regions have their own specialties: you'll find pottery in Mashiko (north of Tokyo), **Bizen** (a specific type of pottery) in Okayama and lacquer-ware (called **shikki**) in Aizu (in Fukushima prefecture), Wajima (in Ishikawa prefecture) and Hida Takayama (in Gifu prefecture). You may also be interested in bamboo products, which are produced throughout Japan.

Antiques

How old is this?	どのくらい古いですか。 dono kurai furui desu ka
Do you have anything of the…era?	…時代のものはありますか。 …jidai no mono wa arimasu ka
Will I have problems with customs?	税関で問題になりますか。 zeekan de mondai ni narimasu ka
Is there a certificate of authenticity?	鑑定書はありますか。 kanteesho wa arimasu ka

Clothing

I'd like…	…が欲しいんですが …ga hoshiin desu ga
Can I try this on?	これを試着できますか。 kore o shichaku dekimasu ka
It doesn't fit.	身体に合いません。 karada ni aimasen
It's too…	…すぎます。 …sugimasu
– big	– 大き ooki
– small	– 小さ chiisa
– short	– 短 mijika
– long	– 長 naga
Do you have this in size…?	これで…サイズのはありますか。 korede… saizu no wa arimasu ka
Do you have this in a *bigger/smaller* size?	もう少し 大きい／小さい のがありますか。 moo sukoshi *ookii/chiisai* no ga arimasu ka

▶ For numbers, see page 161.

You May See...

紳士服	men's clothing
婦人服	women's clothing
子供服	children's clothing

Color

I'm looking for something in…	…のを探しているんですが。 …no o sagashite irun desu ga
– beige	– ベージュ beeju
– black	– 黒い kuroi
– blue	– ブルー buruu
– brown	– 茶色 chairo
– green	– グリーン guriin
– gray [grey]	– グレー guree
– orange	– オレンジ色 orenji iro
– pink	– ピンク pinku
– purple	– 紫 murasaki
– red	– 赤い akai
– white	– 白い shiroi
– yellow	– 黄色 kiiro

Clothes and Accessories

backpack	リュックサック ryukkusakku
belt	ベルト beruto
bikini	ビキニ bikini
blouse	ブラウス burausu
bra	ブラジャー burajaa
coat	コート kooto
dress	ワンピース wanpiisu
hat	帽子 booshi
jacket	上着 uwagi
jeans	ジーパン jiipan
pajamas	パジャマ pajama

pants [trousers]	ズボン zubon
panty hose [tights]	パンスト pansuto
purse [handbag]	ハンドバッグ handobaggu
raincoat	レインコート einkooto
scarf	スカーフ sukaafu
shirt (men's)	ワイシャツ waishatsu
shorts	半ズボン hanzubon
skirt	スカート sukaato
socks	靴下 kutsushita
suit	スーツ suutsu
sunglasses	サングラス sangurasu
sweater	セーター seetaa
sweatshirt	トレーナー toreenaa
swimsuit	水着 *mizugi*
T-shirt	Tシャツ tii shatsu
tie	ネクタイ nekutai
underpants	パンツ pantsu

Fabric

I'd like...	...が欲しいんですが ...ga hoshiin desu ga
– cotton	– 綿/コットン *men/kotton*
– denim	– デニム denimu
– lace	– レース reesu
– leather	– 革 kawa

– linen	– 麻 asa
– silk	– 絹 kinu
– wool	– ウール uuru
Is it machine washable?	洗濯機で洗えますか。sentakuki de araemasu ka

Shoes

I'd like...	...が欲しいんですが ...ga hoshiin desu ga
– *high-heeled/flat* shoes	– ハイヒール／平らな靴 haihiiru/taira na kutsu
– boots	– ブーツ buutsu
– loafers	– ローファー roofaa
– sandals	– サンダル sandaru
– shoes	– 靴 kutsu
– slippers	– スリッパ surippa
– sneakers	– スニーカー suniikaa
In size...	サイズ…の saizu...no

▶ For numbers, see page 161.

Sizes

small (S)	小 shoo
medium (M)	中 chuu
large (L)	大 dai
extra large (XL)	特大 tokudai
petite	ペティート petiito
plus size	プラス purasu

Newsstand and Tobacconist

Do you sell English-language *books/newspapers*?	英語の本/新聞はありますか。 eego no *hon/shinbun* wa arimasu ka
I'd like...	...が欲しいんですが ...ga hoshiin desu ga
– candy [sweets]	– キャンデー kyandee
– chewing gum	– ガム gamu
– a chocolate bar	– チョコレート chokoreeto
– cigars	– 葉巻 hamaki
– a *pack/carton* of cigarettes	– 煙草 一箱／一カートン tabako *hitohako/ichi kaaton*
– a lighter	– ライター raitaa
– a magazine	– 雑誌 zasshi
– matches	– マッチ matchi
– a newspaper	– 新聞 shinbun
– a pen	– ボールペン boorupen
– a postcard	– 絵葉書 ehagaki
– a *road/town* map of...	– 道路／市街地図 *dooro/shigai* chizu
– stamps	– 切手 kitte

Photography

I'm looking for a(n)... camera.	...カメラを探しているんですが。 ...kamera o sagashite irun desu ga
– automatic	– オートマチック ootomachikku
– digital	– デジタル dejitaru
– disposable	– 使い捨て tsukaisute

I'd like…	…が欲しいんですが …ga hoshiin desu ga
– a battery	– 電池 denchi
– digital prints	– デジタルカメラプリント dejitaru kamera purinto
– a memory card	– メモリーカード memorii kaado
Can I print digital photos here?	デジタル写真をプリントできますか。dejitaru shashin o purinto dekimasu ka

Sports and Leisure

Essential

When's the game?	試合はいつですか。shiai wa itsu desu ka
Where's…?	…はどこですか。…wa doko desu ka
– the beach	– ビーチ biichi
– the park	– 公園 kooen
– the pool	– プール puuru
Is it safe to *swim/ dive* here?	ここで泳いでも/飛び込んでも大丈夫ですか。 kokode *oyoidemo/tobikondemo* daijoobu desu ka
Can I rent [hire] golf clubs?	ゴルフクラブを借りたいんですが。gorufu kurabu o karitai n desu ga
How much per hour?	料金は1時間いくらですか。ryookin wa ichijikan ikura desu ka
How far is it to…?	…まで、どのくらいありますか。…made dono kurai arimasu ka
Can you show me on the map?	この地図で教えてください。kono chizu de oshiete kudasai

Spectator Sports

When's…?	…はいつですか。…wa itsu desu ka
– the basketball game	– バスケットボールの試合 basuketto booru no shiai
– the boxing match	– ボクシングの試合 bokushingu no shiai
– the cycling race	– 自転車レース jitensha reesu
– the golf tournament	– ゴルフトーナメント gorufu toonamento
– the soccer [football] game	– サッカーの試合 sakkaa no shiai
– the tennis match	– テニスの試合 tenisu no shiai
– the volleyball game	– バレーボールの試合 bareebooru no shiai
Which teams are playing?	どのチームが出ますか。dono chiimu ga demasu ka
Where's…?	…はどこですか。…wa doko desu ka
– the horsetrack	– 競馬場 keebajoo
– the racetrack	– 競馬場 keebajoo
– the stadium	– スタジアム sutajiamu
Where can I place a bet?	どこで賭け金を払いますか。doko de kakekin o haraimasu ka

Most sports that are popular in the West—such as golf, tennis, football, basketball, etc.—are also popular in Japan. Many cities have martial arts halls in which you can watch **kendoo**, **juudoo**, **aikidoo** and **karate**. Japan's real national sport is **sumoo** (wrestling). This is an ancient, highly ritualized sport providing a true spectacle. There are six tournaments a year, each lasting 15 days. These are held in January, May, and September in Tokyo; in March in Osaka; July in Nagoya; November in Fukuoka. Skiing is also very popular in this mountainous country, and there are numerous ski resorts. It is best to reserve ski accommodations before you leave.

Participating

Where's…?	…はどこですか。…wa doko desu ka
– the golf course	– ゴルフ場 gorufujoo
– the gym	– スポーツジム supootsu jimu
– the park	– 公園 kooen
– the tennis courts	– テニスコート tenisu kooto
How much per…	料金は…いくらですか。ryookin wa …ikura desu ka
– day	– 日 nichi/hi
– hour	– 時間 jikan
– game	– 試合 shiai
– round	– ラウンド raundo
Can I rent [hire]…?	…を借りられますか。…o kariraremasu ka
– golf clubs	– クラブ kurabu
– equipment	– 道具 doogu
– a racket	– ラケット raketto

At the Beach/Pool

Where's the *beach/pool*?	ビーチ／プール はどこですか。 *biichi/puuru* wa doko desu ka
Is there…?	…はありますか。 …wa arimasu ka
– a kiddie pool	－子供用のプール kodomo yoo no puuru
– an *indoor/outdoor* pool	－屋内／屋外プール *okunai/okugai* puuru
– a lifeguard	－プール監視員 puuru kanshiin
Is it safe…?	…大丈夫ですか。 …daijoobu desu ka
– to swim	－泳いでも oyoidemo
– to dive	－飛び込んでも tobikondemo
– for children	－子供に kodomo ni
I want to rent [hire]…	…を借りたいんですが。 …o karitain desu ga
– a deck chair	－デッキチェア dekki chea
– diving equipment	－スキューバダイビング用具 sukyuuba daibingu yoogu
– a jet-ski	－ジェットスキー jetto sukii
– a motorboat	－モーターボート mootaa booto
– a rowboat	－ボート booto
– snorkeling equipment	－シュノーケル shunookeru
– a surfboard	－サーフボード saafuboodo
– a towel	－タオル taoru
– an umbrella	－パラソル parasoru
– water skis	－水上スキー suijoo sukii
– a windsurfer	－ウインドサーフィン uindo saafin
For…hours.	…時間 …jikan

▶For travel with children, see page 141.

Beaches close to Tokyo and Osaka can be very crowded in the summer, and until September 1, when summer officially ends. Okinawa, the Amakusa Islands, the Yaeyama Islands are good for snorkeling and scuba diving.

Sports and Leisure

Winter Sports

A lift pass for *a day/ five days*, please.	1日/5日分のリフト券、お願いします。 *ichinichi/itsuka* bun no rifutoken onegai shimasu
I want to rent [hire]…	…を借りたいんですが。 …o karitain desu ga
– boots	– スキー靴 sukii gutsu
– a helmet	– ヘルメット herumetto
– poles	– ストック sutokku
– skis	– スキー sukii
– a snowboard	– スノーボード sunoo boodo
– snowshoes	– スノーシューズ sunooshuuzu
These are too *big/small*.	大き/小さすぎます。 *ooki/chiisa* sugimasu
Are there lessons?	レッスンがありますか。 ressun ga arimasu ka
I'm a beginner.	初心者です。 shoshinsha desu
I'm experienced.	経験者です。 keekensha desu
A trail [piste] map, please.	ゲレンデマップ、お願いします。 gerende mappu onegai shimasu

You will find opportunities for both downhill and cross-country skiing in Japan. Many travelers choose to combine skiing with the delights of a **ryokan** or **minshuku** (traditional Japanese guest houses) offering a hot spa.

131

You May See...

ケーブルカー	cable car
リフト	chair lift
初心者	novice
中級	intermediate
上級	expert
コース閉鎖中	trail [piste] closed

In the Countryside

I'd like a map of...	...の地図をください。...no chizu o kudasai
– this region	– この地域 kono chiiki
– the walking routes	– ハイキングコース haikingu koosu
– bike routes	– サイクリングコース saikuringu koosu
– the trails	– ハイキング haikingu
Is it *easy/difficult*?	やさしい／難しい ですか。 *yasashii/muzukashii* desu ka
Is it *far/steep*?	遠い／急斜面 ですか。 *tooi/kyuushamen* desu ka
How far is it to...?	...まで、どのくらいありますか。...made dono kurai arimasu ka
Can you show me on the map?	この地図で教えてください。kono chizu de oshiete kudasai
I'm lost.	道に迷いました。michi ni mayoimashita
Where's the...?	...はどこですか。...wa doko desu ka
– bridge	– 橋 hashi
– cave	– 洞窟 dookutsu
– canal	– 運河 unga

– cliff	– 崖 gake
– farmhouse	– 農家 nooka
– field	– 野原 nohara
– forest	– 森 mori
– hill	– 丘 oka
– island	– 島 shima
– lake	– 湖 mizuumi
– mountain	– 山 yama
– mountain pass	– 山道 yama michi
– mountain range	– 山脈 sanmyaku
– nature reserve	– 自然保護区域 shizen hogo kuiki
– panorama	– 展望 tenboo
– park	– 公園 kooen
– peak	– 山頂 sanchoo
– plain	– 平野 heeya
– pond	– 池 ike
– rapids	– 急流 kyuuryuu
– river	– 川 kawa
– hot spring	– 温泉 onsen
– stream	– 小川 ogawa
– valley	– 谷間 tanima
– viewpoint	– 展望台 tenboo dai
– village	– 村 mura
– waterfall	– 滝 taki
– wood	– 林 hayashi

Culture and Nightlife

Essential

What is there to do in the evenings?	夜は何がありますか。 yoru wa nani ga arimasu ka
Do you have a program of events?	催し物のプログラムがありますか。 moyooshimono no puroguramu ga arimasu ka
What's playing at the movies [cinema] tonight?	今晩、どんな映画をやっていますか。 konban donna eega o yatte imasu ka
Where's...?	...はどこですか。 ...wa doko desu ka
– the downtown area	− 繁華街 hankagai
– the bar	− バー baa
– the dance club	− ディスコ disuko
Is there a cover charge?	カバーチャージはありますか。 kabaa chaaji wa arimasu ka

If you are looking for popular music and dancing you'll find good quality jazz clubs and conventional discos, even country-and-western bars, all in Tokyo's cosmopolitan restaurant districts of Akasaka and Roppongi. Teenagers might like to join in the open-air dancing at Harajuku, near Yoyogi Park.

Entertainment

Can you recommend...?	...はありますか。 ...wa arimasu ka
– a concert	− コンサート konsaato
– a movie	− 映画 eega

– an opera	– オペラ opera
– a play	– 芝居 shibai
When does it *start/ end*?	いつ始まりますか／終わりますか。itsu *hajimarimasu ka/owarimasu ka*
What's the dress code?	服装規定がありますか。fukusoo kitei ga arimasu ka
I like...	…が好きです。...ga suki desu
– classical music	– クラシック音楽 kurashikku ongaku
– folk music	– フォーク fooku
– jazz	– ジャズ jazu
– pop music	– ポピュラー音楽 popyuraa ongaku
– rap	– ラップ音楽 rappu ongaku

▶ For ticketing, see page 21.

There are many local and regional festivals throughout the year in Japan. Some examples are; the Snow Festival in Sapporo, from late February to mid-March. In late March to early April the famous Japanese cherry blossoms invite everyone out to enjoy. In May, Kyoto has the Aoi Festival, one of three festivals that reenact Kyoto's history. The other two are the Jidai Festival in October and Gion Festival in July.

You May Hear...

| 携帯電話をお切りください。keitaidenwa o okiri kudasai | Turn off your cell [mobile] phones, please. |

Nightlife

What is there to do in the evenings?	夜は何がありますか。yoru wa nani ga arimasu ka
Can you recommend...?	いい…はありますか。ii...wa arimasu ka
– a bar	– バー baa
– a dance club	– ディスコ disuko
– a gay club	– ゲイバー gee baa
– a jazz club	– ジャズクラブ jazu kurabu
– a club with Japanese music	– 日本の音楽が聴けるクラブ nihon no ongaku ga kikeru kurabu
Is there live music?	生演奏がありますか。nama ensoo ga arimasu ka
How do I get there?	どうやって行くんですか。dooyatte ikun desu ka
Is there a cover charge?	カバーチャージはありますか。kabaa chaaji wa arimasu ka
Let's go dancing.	ダンスをしに行きましょう。dansu o shini ikimashoo

Japan has a wide variety of traditional arts and culture for visitors to enjoy. Some examples from nature are: **bonsai**, an art to recreate nature on a small scale using plants; Japanese gardens, peaceful natural scenes located in cities or temples and **ikebana** or flower arrangement. If you prefer performances, don't miss **bunraku**, puppet theater using dolls of about three feet tall, manipulated by people on the stage. And of course there is **kabuki**, traditional Japanese theater.

Special Needs

Essential

I'm here on business.	仕事で来ました。shigoto de kimashita
Here's my business card.	名刺をどうぞ。meeshi o doozo
Can I have your card?	お名刺をいただけますか。omeeshi o itadakemasu ka
I have a meeting with…	…さんと会うことになっています。…san to aukoto ni natte imasu
Where's…?	…はどこですか。…wa doko desu ka
– the business center	– ビジネス・センター bijinesu sentaa
– the convention hall	– 会議場 kaigijoo
– the meeting room	– 会議室 kaigishitsu

Business Communication

I'm here to attend…	…に出るために来ました。…ni derutame ni kimashita
– a seminar	– セミナー seminaa
– a conference	– 会議 kaigi
– a meeting	– 会議 kaigi
My name is…	…です。…desu
May I introduce my colleague…	同僚の…をご紹介します。dooryoo no …san o goshookai shimasu
I have a *meeting/an appointment* with…	…さんとミーティング／約束があります。…san to *miitingu/yakusoku* ga arimasu
I'm sorry I'm late.	遅くなって済みません。osoku natte sumimasen
I need an interpreter.	通訳をお願いします。tsuuyaku o onegai shimasu

You can reach me at the…Hotel.	…ホテルに連絡してください。…hoteru ni renraku shite kudasai
I'm here until…	…までここにいます。…made kokoni imasu

The exchange of business cards, together with a bow, is the Japanese equivalent of shaking hands, although bowing is not expected of foreign visitors. Visiting cards (**meeshi**) are printed on one side in English and on the other in Japanese. They can be obtained rapidly at most major hotels. Include your occupation or position; if you don't, it will be assumed that your job is of low status.

I need to…	… たいんですが。…tain desu ga
– make a call…	– 電話をかけ denwa o kake
– make a photocopy	– コピーをし kopi o shi
– send an e-mail	– 電子メールを送り denshimeeru o okuri
– send a fax	– ファックスを送り fakkusu o okuri
– send a package (overnight)	– 小包を（翌日配達で）送り kozutsumi o (yokujitsu haitatsu de) okuri
It was a pleasure to meet you.	お目に掛かれてよかったです。ome ni kakarete yokatta desu

▶ For internet and communications, see page 47.

You May Hear…

お約束は承っていますか。oyakusoku wa uketamawatte imasu ka	Do you have an appointment?
お会いになりたいのは？oaini naritai nowa	With whom?
ただ今会議中でございます。tadaima kaigichuu de gozaimasu	*He/She* is in a meeting.
少々お待ちください。shooshoo omachi kudasai	One moment, please.
どうぞお座りください。doozo osuwari kudasai	Have a seat.
何かお飲物はいかがですか。nanika onomimono wa ikaga desu ka	Would you like something to drink?
お越しいただきましてありがとうございました。okosi itadakimashite arigatoo gozaimashita	Thank you for coming.

Travel with Children

Essential

Is there a discount for children?	子供の割引はありますか。 kodomo no waribiki wa arimasu ka
Can you recommend a baby-sitter?	信頼できるベビーシッターを教えてください。 shinrai dekiru bebii shittaa o oshiete kudasai
Could we have a *child's seat/highchair*?	子供用の椅子/ハイチェアをお願いします。 *kodomo yoo no isu/hai chea* o onegai shimasu
Where can I change the baby?	おむつはどこで替えられますか。 omutsu wa doko de kaeraremasu ka

Fun with Kids

Can you recommend something for the kids?	子供が楽しめるところを教えてください。 kodomo ga tanoshimeru tokoro o oshiete kudasai
Where's...?	...はどこですか。 ...wa doko desu ka
– the amusement park	– 遊園地 yuuenchi
– the arcade	– ゲームセンター geemu sentaa
– the kiddie [paddling] pool	– 子供用のプール kodomo yoo no puuru
– the playground	– 公園 kooen
– the zoo	– 動物園 doobutsu en
Are kids allowed?	子供でも入れますか。 kodomo demo hairemasu ka
Is it safe for kids?	子供でも大丈夫ですか。 kodomo demo daijoobu desu ka
Is it suitable for... year olds?	...歳の子供でも大丈夫ですか。 ...sai no kodomo demo daijoobu desu ka

▶ For numbers, see page 161.

かわいい！ kawaii		How cute!
お名前は？ onamae wa		What's his/her name?
何歳ですか。 nansai desu ka		How old is *he/she*?

Basic Needs for Kids

Do you have…?	…は、ありますか。 …wa arimasu ka
– a baby bottle	– 哺乳瓶 honyuubin
– baby wipes	– お尻拭き oshiri fuki
– a car seat	– チャイルドシート chairudo shiito
– a children's menu	– お子さまメニュー okosama menyuu
– a *child's seat/* *highchair*	– 子供用のイス/ハイチェア kodomo yoo no isu/haichea
– a crib	– ベビーベッド bebii beddo
– diapers [nappies]	– (紙)おむつ (kami) omutsu

– formula	– ミルク miruku
– a pacifier [soother]	– おしゃぶり oshaburi
– a playpen	– ベビーサークル bebii saakuru
– a stroller [pushchair]	– 乳母車 ubaguruma

Can I breastfeed the baby here?	ここで授乳してもいいですか。 kokode junyuu shitemo ii desu ka
Where can I change the baby?	おむつはどこで替えられますか。 omutsu wa doko de kaeraremasu ka

▶ For dining with kids, see page 61.

Babysitting

Can you recommend a reliable baby-sitter?	信頼できるベビーシッターを教えてください。 shinrai dekiru bebii shittaa o oshiete kudasai
What's the charge?	料金はいくらですか。 ryookin wa ikura desu ka
I'll pick them up at...	...に迎えに行きます。 ...ni mukae ni ikimasu

▶ For time, see page 164.

I can be reached at...	...に電話してください。 ...ni denwa shite kudasai

Health and Emergency

Can you recommend a pediatrician?	小児科医を教えてください。 shoonikai o oshiete kudasai
My child is allergic to...	うちの子供は...にアレルギーがあります。 uchi no kodomo wa...ni arerugii ga arimasu
My child is missing.	子供がいなくなりました。 kodomo ga inaku narimashita
Have you seen a *boy/girl*?	男／女の子を見ましたか。 *otoko/onna* no ko o mimashita ka

▶ For food items, see page 84.

▶ For health, see page 149.

▶ For police, see page 147.

For the Disabled

Essential

Is there...?	...はありますか。 ...wa arimasu ka
– access for the disabled	– 身体障害者用通路 shintai shogaisha yoo tsuuro
– a wheelchair ramp	– 車椅子用スロープ kuruma isu yoo suroopu
– a handicapped- [disabled-] accessible toilet	– ハンディキャップ用トイレ handikyappu yoo toire
I need...	...が要るんですが。 ...ga irun desu ga
– assistance	– 助け tasuke
– an elevator [lift]	– エレベーター erebeetaa
– a ground–floor room	– 一階の部屋 ikkai no heya

Getting Help

I'm disabled.	私は身体が不自由です。watashi wa karada ga fujiyuu desu
I'm deaf.	私は耳が聞こえません。watashi wa mimi ga kikoemasen
I'm *visually/hearing* impaired.	私は目がよく見えません／耳がよく聞こえません。watashi wa *me ga yoku miemasen/mimi ga yoku kikoemasen*
I'm unable to *walk far/use the stairs*.	私は遠くまで歩けません／階段を上れません。watashi wa *tooku made arukemasen/kaidan o noboremasen*
Can I bring my wheelchair?	車椅子を持っていってもいいですか。kurumaisu o motte ittemo ii desu ka
Are guide dogs permitted?	盲導犬が入ってもいいですか。moodooken ga haittemo ii desu ka
Can you help me?	助けてください。tasukete kudasai
Please *open/hold* the door.	ドアを開けて／開けておいてください。doa o *akete/akete oite* kudasai

i Many provincial main stations have elevators and other facilities for disabled travelers. However, smaller stations generally do not.

145

▼ Resources

Emergencies

Essential

Help!	助けて！tasukete
Go away!	あっちへ行け！atchi e ike
Call the police!	警察を呼んで！keesatsu o yonde
Stop thief!	泥棒！doroboo
Get a doctor!	医者を呼んで！isha o yonde
Fire!	火事だ！kaji da
I'm lost.	道に迷いました。michi ni mayoimashita
Can you help me?	助けてください。tasukete kudasai

Police

Essential

Call the police!	警察を呼んで！keesatsu o yonde
Where's the police station?	交番はどこですか。kooban wa doko desu ka
There has been an *accident/attack*.	事故がありました／襲われました。jiko ga arimashita/osowaremashita
My child is missing.	子供がいなくなりました。kodomo ga inaku narimashita
I need an interpreter.	通訳が要るんですが。tsuuyaku ga irun desu ga
I need...	…したいんですが。...shitain desu ga
– to contact my lawyer	– 弁護士に連絡 bengoshi ni renraku
– to make a phone call	– 電話 denwa
I'm innocent.	無実です。mujitsu desu

147

You May Hear...

この用紙に記入してください。	kono yooshi ni kinyuu shite kudasai	Please fill out this form.
身分証明書を見せてください。	mibun shoomeisho o misete kudasai	Your identification, please.
いつ／どこで 起きたんですか。	*itsu/dokode* okitan desu ka	*When/Where* did it happen?
どんな顔をしていますか。	donna kao o shite iamsu ka	What does *he/she* look like?

▶ For emergency numbers, see page 53.

Lost Property and Theft

I want to report...	...を報告したいんですが。	...o hookoku shitain desu ga
– a mugging	– 強盗	gootoo
– a rape	– レイプ	reepu
– a theft	– 泥棒	doroboo
I've been mugged.	強盗にあいました。	gootoo ni aimashita
I've lost my...	...をなくしました。	...o nakushimashita
My...has been stolen.	...を盗まれました。	...o nusumaremashita
– backpack	– リュックサック	ryukkusakku
– bicycle	– 自転車	jitensha
– camera	– カメラ	kamera
– car	– 車	kuruma
– rental car	– レンタカー	renta kaa
– computer	– コンピュータ	konpyuuta
– credit cards	– クレジットカード	kurejitto kaado
– jewelry	– 宝石	hooseki

– money	– お金 okane
– passport	– パスポート pasupooto
– purse/wallet	– 財布 saifu
– traveler's checks [cheques]	– トラベラーズチェック toraberaazu chekku
I need a police report for my insurance claim.	保険の申請に警察の証明書が要ります。 hoken no shinsee ni keesatsu no shoomeesho ga irimasu

Health

Essential

I'm ill.	具合が悪いんです。 guai ga waruin desu
I need an English-speaking doctor.	英語ができる医者はいますか。 eego ga dekiru isha wa imasu ka
It hurts here.	ここが痛いんです。 koko ga itain desu
I have a stomachache.	お腹が痛いんです。 onaka ga itain desu

Finding a Doctor

Can you recommend a *doctor/dentist*?	医者／歯医者を教えてください。 *isha/haisha* o oshiete kudasai
Could the doctor come to see me here?	往診してくれますか。 ooshin shite kuremasu ka
I need an English-speaking doctor.	英語ができる医者はいますか。 eego ga dekiru isha wa imasu ka

What are the office hours?	診察時間はいつですか。shinsatsu jikan wa itsu desu ka
Can I make an appointment…?	…予約したいんですが。…yoyaku shitain desu ga
– for today	– 今日 kyoo
– for tomorrow	– 明日 ashita
– as soon as possible	– できるだけ早く dekirudake hayaku
It's urgent.	至急お願いします。shikyuu onegai shimasu

Symptoms

I'm…	しています。shite imasu
– bleeding	– 出血 shukketsu
– constipated	– 便秘 benpi
– dizzy	– 目眩 memai
I'm *nauseous/ vomiting.*	吐きそうです/吐いています。hakisoo desu/ haite imasu
It hurts here.	ここが痛いんです。koko ga itai n desu

I have…	…があります。…ga arimasu
– an allergic reaction	– アレルギー反応 arerugii hannoo ga
– chest pain	– 胸の痛み mune no itami
– an earache	– 耳の痛み mimi no itami
– a fever	– 熱 netsu
– pain	– 痛み itami
– a rash	– 発疹 hasshin
– some swelling	– 腫れ hare
I have a sprain.	ねんざしました。nenza shimashita
I have a stomachache.	お腹が痛いんです。onaka ga itain desu
I have sunstroke.	日射病にかかりました。nisshabyoo ni kakarimashita
I've been sick [ill] for…days	…日間，病気です。…nichikan byooki desu

▶For numbers, see page 161.

Health Conditions

I'm…	…です。…desu
– anemic	– 貧血症 hinketsu shoo
– diabetic	– 糖尿病 toonyoo byoo
– asthmatic	– ぜんそく zensoku
I'm allergic to *antibiotics/penicillin.*	抗生物質／ペニシリンにアレルギーです。*koosei busshitsu/penishirin* ni arerugii desu

▶For food items, see page 84.

I have arthritis.	関節炎にかかっています。kansetsuen ni kakatte imasu
I have (high/low) blood pressure.	高／低 血圧です。*koo/tei* ketsuatsu desu

| I have a heart condition. | 心臓が悪いんです。shinzoo ga waruin desu |
| I'm on… | …を飲んで います。…o nonde imasu |

You May Hear…

どうしましたか。doo shimashita ka	What's wrong?
どこが痛みますか。doko ga itamimasu ka	Where does it hurt?
ここが痛みますか。koko ga itamimasu ka	Does it hurt here?
他に薬を飲んでいますか。hokani kusuri o nonde imasu ka	Are you taking any other medication?
何かのアレルギーはありますか。nanka no arerugii wa arimasu ka	Are you allergic to anything?
口を開けてください。kuchi o akete kudasai	Open your mouth.
深呼吸してください。shin kokyuu shite kudasai	Breathe deeply.
病院に行ってください。byooin ni itte kudasai	I want you to go to the hospital.

Hospital

Please notify my family.	家族に知らせてください。kazoku ni shirasete kudasai
I'm in pain.	痛みます。itamimasu
I need a *doctor/nurse*.	医者／看護師を呼んでください。*isha/kangoshi* o yonde kudasai
When are visiting hours?	面会時間はいつですか。menkai jikan wa itsu desu ka
I'm visiting…	…の見舞いに来ました。…no mimai ni kimashita

Dentist

I've *broken a tooth/ lost a filling*.	歯を折りました／詰め物をなくしました。ha o orimashita/tsumemono o nakushimashita
I have a toothache.	歯が痛いんです。ha ga itain desu
Can you fix this denture?	この入れ歯を直せますか。kono ireba o naosemasu ka

Gynecologist

I have *menstrual cramps/a vaginal infection*.	生理痛／膣感染症があります。 *seeritsuu/chitsu kansen shoo* ga arimasu
I missed my period	生理がありませんでした。seeri ga arimasen deshita
I'm on the Pill.	ピルを飲んでいます。piru o nonde imasu
I'm *pregnant/not pregnant*.	妊娠して います／いません。ninshin shite *imasu/ imasen*
I haven't had my period for…months.	生理が…ヶ月間ありません。seeri ga… kagetsukan arimasen

Optician

I've lost…	…をなくしました。…o nakushimashita
– one of my contact lenses	– 片方のコンタクトレンズ katahoo no kontakuto renzu
– my glasses	– 眼鏡 megane
– a lens	– レンズ renzu

Payment and Insurance

How much?	いくら ikura
Can I pay by credit card?	クレジットカードを使えますか。kurejitto kaado o tsukaemasu ka
I have insurance.	保険に入っています。hoken ni haitte imasu
Can I have a receipt for my insurance?	保険申請のためにレシートをください。hoken shinsee no tame ni reshiito o kudasai

Pharmacy [Chemist]

Essential

Where's the nearest (all-night) pharmacy?	(夜間営業の) 薬局はどこですか。(yakan eegyoo no) yakkyoku wa doko desu ka
What time does the pharmacy *open/close*?	薬局は何時に開き/閉まりますか。yakkyoku wa nanji ni *aki/shimari* masu ka
What would you recommend for...?	...には何がいいですか。...niwa nani ga ii desu ka
How much should I take?	どのくらい飲むんですか。dono kurai nomun desu ka
Can you fill [make up] this prescription for me?	この薬をください。kono kusuri o kudasai
I'm allergic to...	私は...にアレルギーです。watashi wa...ni arerugii desu

i You will find a large selection of imported medications at the American Pharmacy in Tokyo. These can be more expensive than at home, so if you have any special medical needs it is best to bring an ample supply with you.

Dosage Instructions

How much should I take?	どのくらい飲むんですか。dono kurai nomun desu ka
How many times a day should I take it?	一日何回飲むんですか。ichinichi nankai nomun desu ka
Is it suitable for children?	子供でも飲めますか。kodomo demo nomemasu ka
I'm taking…	…を飲んでいます。…o nonde imasu
Are there side effects?	副作用はありますか。fukusayoo wa arimasu ka

You May See…

一日一回／三回	*once/three times* a day
錠	tablet(s)
滴	drop
ティースプーン／茶さじ	teaspoon(s)
食前／食後／食事中	*before/after/with* meals
空腹時	on an empty stomach
丸ごと飲み下し	swallow whole
眠気を催すことがあります	may cause drowsiness
外用薬	for external use only

Health Problems

I'd like some medicine for…	…の薬をください。…no kusuri o kudasai
– a cold	– 風邪 kaze
– a cough	– 咳 seki
– diarrhea	– 下痢 geri

I'd like some medicine for...	...の薬をください。...no kusuri o kudasai
– insect bites	– 虫刺され mushi sasare
– motion [travel] sickness	– 乗物酔 norimono yoi
– a sore throat	– 喉の痛み nodo no itami
– sunburn	– 日焼け hiyake
– an upset stomach	– 胃 i

Basic Needs

I'd like...	...が欲しいんですが ...ga hoshiin desu ga
– acetaminophen [paracetamol]	– アセタミノーフェン asetaminoofen
– antiseptic cream	– 傷薬 kizugusuri
– aspirin	– 頭痛薬 zutsuuyaku
– bandages	– 包帯 hootai
– a comb	– 櫛 kushi
– condoms	– コンドーム kondoomu
– contact lens solution	– コンタクトレンズ液 kontakutorenzu eki
– deodorant	– デオドラント deodoranto
– a hairbrush	– ヘアブラシ heaburashi
– hair spray	– ヘアスプレー hea supuree
– ibuprofen	– イブプロフェン ibupurofen
– insect repellent	– 防虫剤 boochuuzai
– a nail file	– ネイルファイル neirufairu
– a (disposable) razor	– (使い捨て)カミソリ (tsukaisuite) kamisori
– razor blades	– カミソリの刃 kamisori no ha
– sanitary napkins [pads]	– 生理用ナプキン seeri yoo napukin

– shampoo/ conditioner	－シャンプー/コンディショナー shanpuu/kondishonaa
– soap	－石鹸 sekken
– sunscreen	－日焼け止めクリーム hiyake dome kuriimu
– tampons	－タンポン tanpon
– tissues	－ティッシュペーパー tisshu peepaa
– toilet paper	－トイレットペーパー toiretto peepaa
– toothpaste	－歯磨き粉 hamigakiko

▶ For baby products, see page 142.

Reference

Grammar

Regular Verbs

At first glance Japanese verbs are very straightforward, with only present and past tenses and no special form to indicate person or number. Future tense is gauged from the context.

However, verbs are subject to other changes to express variety of degrees of politeness and mood. The two basic verb forms are:

taberu	to eat	**nomu**	to drink
tabemasu	to eat (polite form)	**nomimasu**	to drink (polite form)

This phrase book uses the polite form throughout.

tabemasu	(I, you, he, she, we, they) eat
tabemasen	(I, you, he, she, we, they) don't/doesn't eat
tabemashita	(I, you, he, she, we, they) ate
tabemasendeshita	(I, you, he, she, we, they) didn't eat

In addition to the above forms, verbs can indicate such functions as causative, command, conditional, passive, potential etc. by adding appropriate suffixes. For example:

tabesasemasu	I cause (someone) to eat
tabero!	Eat!
tabereba	if you eat...

Particles

Japanese uses a number of particles to mark the use, or add to the meaning of the word they follow in a sentence.

ga	subject marker	nodo ga itai desu	literal meaning: The throat is sore.
wa	attention-directing marker	watashi wa nodo ga itai desu	literal meaning: As for me the throat is sore.
o	object marker	gohan o tabemasu	literal meaning: I eat rice.

Irregular Verbs

Japanese has only two irregular verbs: **suru** (to do) and **kuru** (to come). Their polite forms are as follows:

shimasu	do	kimasu	come
shimasen	don't/doesn't do	kimasen	don't/doesn't come
shimashita	did	kimashita	came
shimasendeshita	didn't do	kimasendeshita	didn't come

Nouns and Articles

Japanese nouns have no articles, and no plurals. All nouns have one single form which does not change according to the noun's role in a sentence.

Personal pronouns are used sparingly in Japanese. Use the person's name + **san** instead of a pronoun, or omit the pronoun completely if it is clear who is being addressed or referred to. Personal pronouns are:

watashi	I	**anata*** (singular)	you
watashi tachi	we	**anatagata*** (plural)	you

* These pronouns are very familiar and appropriate only between husband and wife or boyfriend and girlfriend.

Word Order

Japanese questions are formed by adding the particle **ka** (a verbal question mark) to the verb at the end of a sentence. Note that in Japanese the verb always comes last. The basic rule for word order within a sentence is: subject - object - verb

Watashi wa Smith desu.	I'm (Mr./Mrs.) Smith.
Honda-san* desu ka?	Are you (Mr./Mrs.) Honda?

* When addressing a Japanese person you should use the family name followed by san. (Do not use san when referring to yourself!)

Imperatives

There are many ways to indicate an order, depending on how strong you would like it to be. Following is an example of imperative from mild to strong:

Go!	**Itte**	**Ikinasai**	**Ike**

Comparative and Superlative

Unlike English, Japanese adjectives do not indicate comparative or superlative. Instead Japanese employs the following pattern:

Comparative: A **to** B **to dochira ga** adjective **desuka?**

Tookyoo to Oosaka to dochira ga ookii desu ka.

Which is bigger, Tokyo or Osaka?

Superlative: **A to B to C de A ga ichiban** adjective **desu**.

Tookyoo to Oosaka to Kyooto de Tookyoo ga ichiban ookii desu.

Among Tokyo, Osaka and Kyoto, Tokyo is the biggest.

Possessive Pronouns

To make possessive pronouns, use the grammar marker **no** following the person's name or the personal pronoun.

Honda-san no hon	Mr./Mrs. Honda's book
Watashi no hon	my book

Adjectives

A Japanese adjective ends in **–i** and modifies a noun that is placed immediately after it. For example, "a big room" will be **ookii heya**. Japanese adjectives are very different from their English counterparts, and behave more like verbs. The past tense of most adjectives is formed by adding **-katta** to the basic stem:

takai	expensive	**yasui**	cheap
takakatta	(was) expensive	**yasukatta**	(was) cheap

There is another group of adjectives that takes **–na** at the end of the word to modify a noun.

Example: **kiree-na hana** (pretty flower), **taisetsu-na mono** (an important thing), **shizuka-na tokoro** (a quiet place).

Adverbs

An adverb describes a verb. Many Japanese adverbs end in **–ku**, and are derived from adjectives by replacing the final **–i** of an adjective with **–ku**.

Example: **Hayaku hashirimashita.** He ran quickly.

Numbers

Essential

0	零/ゼロ ree/zero
1	一 ichi
2	二 ni
3	三 san
4	四 shi/yon
5	五 go
6	六 roku
7	七 shichi/nana
8	八 hachi
9	九 kyuu/ku
10	十 juu
11	十一 juuichi
12	十二 juuni
13	十三 juusan
14	十四 juushi/juuyon
15	十五 juugo
16	十六 juuroku
17	十七 juushichi/juunana
18	十八 juuhachi
19	十九 juukyuu/juuku
20	二十 nijuu
21	二十一 nijuuichi
22	二十二 nijuuni
30	三十 sanjuu

31	三十一 sanjuuichi
40	四十 yonjuu/shijuu
50	五十 gojuu
60	六十 rokujuu
70	七十 nanajuu/shichijuu
80	八十 hachijuu
90	九十 kyuujuu
100	百 hyaku
101	百一 hyakuichi
200	二百 nihyaku
500	五百 gohyaku
1,000	千 sen
10,000	一万 ichiman
1,000,000	百万 hyakuman

Ordinal Numbers

first	一番 ichiban
second	二番 niban
third	三番 sanban
fourth	四番 yonban
fifth	五番 goban
once	一回 ikkai
twice	二回 nikai
three times	三回 sankai

i In Japanese, there are two ways of counting to ten. There are general numbers (listed on page 161) used for talking about sums of money, telephone numbers, etc. There is also a system for combining a number with an object-specific counter. This system groups objects into types according to shape and size. There are specific ways of counting flat objects, animals, people, etc. Luckily the counter system only applies to numbers from 1-10. After 10 the general number is used. When you are not sure of the correct counter, you can always use the "all-purpose" counters listed below.

"All-purpose" Counters (Numbers 1 - 10)

These counters are strictly used to count "unclassifiable" objects (objects where shape or size are difficult to determine). When you don't know the specific counter use:

1	**hitotsu**	2	**futatsu**
3	**mittsu**	4	**yottsu**
5	**itsutsu**	6	**muttsu**
7	**nanatsu**	8	**yattsu**
9	**kokonotsu**	10	**too**

Other Counters

Flat objects (stamps, paper, etc.)

1	**ichimai**	6	**rokumai**
2	**nimai**	7	**nanamai/shichimai**
3	**sanmai**	8	**hachimai**
4	**yonmai**	9	**kyuumai**
5	**gomai**	10	**juumai**

People

1	hitori	6	rokunin
2	futari	7	nananin/shichinin
3	sannin	8	hachinin
4	yonin	9	kyuunin
5	gonin	10	juunin

Long, thin objects (pen, bottle, umbrella, etc.)

1	ippon	6	roppon
2	nihon	7	nanahon
3	sanbon	8	happon
4	yonhon	9	kyuuhon
5	gohon	10	juppon

For example, the counter for a bottle is **nihon**.

I'd like two bottles of beer.   **Biru o nihon kudasai.**

If you didn't know the counter, you could use the "all-purpose" counter:

I'd like two bottles of beer.   **Biiru o futatsu kudasai.**

Note that the counter usually follows the word it qualifies.

Time

Essential

What time is it?	何時ですか。 nanji desu ka
It's noon [midday].	十二時（正午）です。 juuniji (shoogo) desu
At midnight.	真夜中に mayonaka ni

From nine o'clock to 5 o'clock.	9時から5時まで kuji kara goji made
Twenty [after] past four	四時二十分 yoji nijuppun
A quarter to nine	九時十五分前 kuji juugofun mae
5:30 *a.m./p.m.*	午前／午後 五時 三十分 *gozen/gogo* goji sanjuppun

i In ordinary conversation, time is expressed as shown above. For airline and train timetables, however, the 24-hour clock is used.

Japan is nine hours ahead of GMT all year round. Japan does not change its clocks to reflect winter and summer time.

Days

Sunday	日曜日 nichiyoobi
Monday	月曜日 getsuyoobi
Tuesday	火曜日 kayoobi
Wednesday	水曜日 suiyoobi
Thursday	木曜日 mokuyoobi
Friday	金曜日 kinyoobi
Saturday	土曜日 doyoobi

Japan changed from lunar calendar to the Gregorian calender in 1873. However, the lunar calendar is still used in farming, and in other activities in rural areas of Japan. Japanese calendars start with Sunday and end with Saturday.

Dates

yesterday	昨日 kinoo
today	今日 kyoo
tomorrow	明日 ashita
day	日 nichi/hi
week	週 shuu
month	月 tsuki
year	年 toshi

Dates in Japan are written in Year-Month-Day format. January 1st, 2010 would be 2010 年 1 月 1 日 **nisen juu nen ichi gatsu tsuitachi**, or 2010, January, first.

Months

January	一月 ichigatsu
February	二月 nigatsu
March	三月 sangatsu
April	四月 shigatsu
May	五月 gogatsu
June	六月 rokugatsu
July	七月 shichigatsu
August	八月 hachigatsu
September	九月 kugatsu
October	十月 juugatsu
November	十一月 juuichigatsu
December	十二月 juunigatsu

Seasons

the spring	春 haru
the summer	夏 natsu
the fall [autumn]	秋 aki
the winter	冬 fuyu

Holidays

Public holidays

January 1 **ganjitsu/gantan** New Year's Day

Second Monday in January **seejin no hi** Adult's Day

February 11 **kenkoku kinen no hi** National Foundation Day

March 21* **shunbun no hi** Vernal Equinox Day

April 29 **midori no hi** Greenery Day

May 3 **kenpoo kinen bi** Constitution Day

May 5 **kodomo no hi** Children's Day

September 15 **keeroo no hi** Respect for the Aged Day

September 23* **shuubun no hi** Autumnal Equinox Day

October 10 **taiiku no hi** Health-Sports Day

November 3 **bunka no hi** Culture Day

November 23 **kinroo kansha no hi** Labor Thanksgiving Day

December 23 **tennoo tanjoobi** Emperor's Birthday

* These dates are lunar and change year by year.

The most important holiday in Japan is New Year's day. All the stores are closed on the January first, and some will close on the second and third as well. Adult's Day (second Monday in January) is designated to celebrate those who are and will be 20 during the year. The week from Greenery Day (April 29) to Children's Day (May 5) is called the Golden Week. Many people take advantage of the four holidays falling during this week (Greenery Day, May Day, Constitution Day, and Children's Day) to travel, thus creating traffic jams everywhere. Bon Festival, from August 13 to 16, is a time when many people go to their ancestral home: the souls of the deceased ancestors are considered to come home during this time.

Conversion Tables

Mileage

1 km – 0.62 mi	20 km – 12.4 mi
5 km – 3.10 mi	50 km – 31.0 mi
10 km – 6.20 mi	100 km – 61.0 mi

Measurement

1 gram	グラム guramu	= 1000 milligrams	= 0.035 oz.
1 kilogram (kg)	キログラム kiroguramu	= 1000 grams	= 2.2 lb
1 liter (l)	リットル rittoru	= 1000 milliliters	= 1.06 U.S./0.88 Brit. quarts
1 centimeter (cm)	センチ senta	= 10 millimeters	= 0.4 inch
1 meter (m)	メートル meetoru	= 100 centimeters	= 39.37 inches/ 3.28 feet
1 kilometer (km)	キロメート ル kiromeetoru	= 1000 meters	= 0.62 mile

Temperature

-40° C – -40° F	1° C – 30° F	20° C – 68° F
-30° C – -22° F	0° C – 32° F	25° C – 77° F
-20° C – -4° F	5° C – 41° F	30° C – 86° F
-10° C – 14° F	10° C – 50° F	35° C – 95° F
-5° C – 23° F	15° C – 59° F	

Oven Temperature

100° C – 212° F	177° C – 350° F
121° C – 250° F	204° C – 400° F
149° C – 300° F	204° C – 400° F

Useful Websites

For airport safety information
www.tsa.gov (USA)
www.caa.co.uk (U.K.)

For general tourism information about Japan
www.japan-guide.com
www.japantravelinfo.com

For Japanese tourist information offices
www.jnto.go.jp
www.visitjapan.jp
www.itcj.or.jp

Gay-friendly travel in Japan
www.gay.com/travel/destinations

For hostel reservations and information
www.hihostels.com

For information about driving in Japan
www.japandriverslicense.com

English–Japanese Dictionary

A

a.m. 午前 gozen

abbey 修道院 shuudooin

access v (Internet) アクセスします akusesu shimasu

accident 事故 kootsuu jiko

accommodation 宿泊設備 shukuhaku setsubi

account n 会計 kaikee

acupuncture 鍼 hari

adapter アダプタ adaputa

address 住所 juusho

after …の後 …no ato

afternoon 午後 gogo

aftershave アフターシェーブ afutaa sheebu

age 年齢 nenree

agency 代理店 dairiten

AIDS エイズ eezu

air conditioning エアコン eakon

air pump エアポンプ eaponpu

airline 航空会社 kookuu gaisha

airmail 航空便 kookuubin

airplane 飛行機 hikooki

airport 空港 kuukoo

aisle 通路 tsuuro

aisle seat 通路側の座席 tsuurogawa no zaseki

allergic アレルギー arerugii

allergic reaction アレルギー反応 arerugii hannoo

alone 一人の人 hitori no hito

alter v (clothing) 直します naoshi masu

alternate route 他の道 hoka no michi

aluminum foil アルミホイル arumi hoiru

amazing すごい sugoi

ambulance 救急車 kyuukyuusha

American アメリカの amerika no

amusement park 遊園地 yuuenchi

anemic 貧血の hinketsu no

anesthesia 麻酔 masui

animal 動物 doobutsu

ankle 足首 ashikubi

antibiotic 抗生物質 koosee busshitsu

antiques store 骨董店 kottooten

antiseptic cream 傷薬 kizugusuri

anything 何でも nandemo

apartment マンション manshon

appendix (body part) 盲腸 moochoo

appetizer おつまみ otsumami

appointment 予約 yoyaku

arcade アーケード aakeedo

area code 市外局番 shigai kyokuban

arm 腕 ude

adj	adjective	BE	British English	n	noun
v	verb				

aromatherapy アロマセラピー aroma serapii

around (the corner) 道を曲がったところ michi o magatta tokoro

arrivals (airport) 到着 toochaku

arrive V着きます tsuki masu

artery 動脈 doomyaku

arthritis 関節炎 kansetsuen

Asian アジアの ajia no

aspirin 頭痛薬 zutsuuyaku

asthmatic 喘息の zensoku no

ATM キャッシュコーナー kyasshu koonaa

attack 襲います osoimasu

attend V出席します shusseki shimasu

attraction (place) アトラクション atorakushon

attractive 魅力的 miryokuteki

Australian オーストラリア人 oosutorariajin

automatic 自動 jidoo

automatic car オートマチック ootomachikku

B

baby 赤ちゃん akachan

baby bottle 哺乳瓶 honyuubin

baby wipe おしりふき oshirifuki

babysitter ベビーシッター bebii shittaa

back (body part) 背中 senaka

backpack リュックサック ryukkusakku

bag バッグ baggu

baggage [BE] 荷物 nimotsu

baggage claim 手荷物引渡所 tenimotsu hikiwatashijo

baggage ticket 手荷物引換証 tenimotsu hikikaeshoo

bakery パン屋 pan-ya

ballet バレエ baree

bandage 包帯 hootai

bank 銀行 ginkoo

bar バー baa

barber 床屋 tokoya

baseball 野球 yakyuu

basket (grocery store) かご kago

basketball バスケットボール basuketto booru

bathroom 風呂場 furoba

bathroom (toilet) トイレ toire

battery 電池 denchi

battleground 戦場跡 senjooato

beach 海岸／ビーチ kaigan/biichi

beautiful 美しい utsukushii

bed ベッド beddo

begin V始めます hajime masu

before 前 mae

beginner 初心者 shoshinsha

behind 後ろ ushiro

beige ベージュ beeju

belt ベルト beruto

berth 寝台 shindai

best 一番いい ichiban ii

better もっといい motto ii

bicycle 自転車 jitensha

big 大きい ookii

bigger もっと大きい motto ookii

bike route 自転車ルート jitensha ruuto

bikini ビキニ bikini

bill v(charge) 請求します seekyuu shimasu; ~ n (money) 紙幣 shihee; ~ n (of sale) 請求書 seekyuusho; itemized ~ 明細書 meesaisho

bird 鳥 tori

birthday 誕生日 tanjoobi

black 黒い kuroi

bladder 膀胱 bookoo

bland 味が薄い aji ga usui

blanket 毛布 moofu

bleed v出血します shukketsu shimasu

blood 血液 ketsueki

blood pressure 血圧 ketsuatsu

blouse ブラウス burausu

blue ブルー buruu

board v(plane) 搭乗します toojoo shimasu, (train) 乗車します joosha shimasu

boarding pass 搭乗券 toojoo ken

boat ボート booto

bone 骨 hone

book 本 hon

bookstore 本屋 hon-ya

boots ブーツ buutu

boring つまらない tsumaranai

botanical garden 植物園 shokubutsuen

bother v邪魔します jama shimasu

bottle 瓶 bin

bottle opener 栓抜き sennuki

bowl ボール booru

box 箱 hako

boy 男の子 otoko noko

boyfriend ボーイフレンド booi furendo

bra ブラジャー burajaa

bracelet ブレスレット buresuretto

brakes (car) ブレーキ bureeki

break v 折れます oremasu

break-in (burglary) 侵入します shin-nyuu shimasu

breakdown 故障 koshoo

breakfast 朝食 chooshoku

breast 乳房 chibusa

breastfeed 母乳をあげます bonyuu o agemasu

breathe v呼吸します kokyuu shimasu

bridge 橋 hashi

briefs (clothing) ブリーフ buriifu

bring (people) v連れてきます tsurete kimasu; (things) 持ってきます motte kimasu

British イギリス人 igirisujin

broken 壊れた kowareta

brooch ブローチ buroochi

broom 箒 hooki

brother (my older) 兄 ani

brother (my younger) 弟 otooto

brother (someone else's older) お兄さん oniisan

brother (someone else's younger) 弟さん otootosan

brown 茶色 chairo

bug 虫 mushi

building ビル／建物 biru/tatemono

burn v 焼きます yakimasu

bus バス basu

bus station バスターミナル basu taaminaru

bus stop バス停留所／バス停 basu teeryuujo/basutee

bus ticket バスの切符 basu no kippu

bus tour バス旅行 basu ryokoo

business 仕事 shigoto

business card 名刺 meeshi

business center ビジネス・センター bijinesu sentaa

business class ビジネス・クラス bijinesu kurasu

business hours 営業時間 eegyoo jikan

butcher 肉屋 nikuya

buttocks お尻 oshiri

buy v 買います kaimasu

bye ごめんください gomen kudasai

C

cabin キャビン kyabin

cable car ケーブル・カー keeburu kaa

café 喫茶店 kissaten

call v 電話します denwa shimasu

calligraphy supplies 習字用具 shuuji yoogu

calories カロリー karorii

camera カメラ kamera

camp v キャンプします kyanpu shimasu; no ~ing キャンプ禁止 kyanpu kinshi

campsite キャンプ場 kyanpujoo

can opener 缶切り kankiri

Canada カナダ kanada

Canadian カナダ人 kanadajin

cancel v キャンセルします kyanseru shimasu

candy キャンデー kyandee

canned good 缶詰 kanzume

canyon 峡谷 kyookoku

car 車 kuruma

car hire [BE] レンタカー rentakaa

car park [BE] 駐車場 chuushajoo

car rental レンタカー rentakaa

car seat チャイルドシート chairudo shiito

carafe カラフ karafu

card カード kaado

carry-on 手荷物 tenimotsu

cart カート kaato

carton カートン kaaton

case (amount) ケース keesu

cash v 換金します kankin shimasu; ~ n 現金 genkin

cash advance キャッシング・サービス kyasshingu saabisu

cashier 会計 kaikee

casino カジノ kajino

castle お城 oshiro

cathedral 大聖堂 daiseedoo

cave 洞窟 dookutsu

CD CD shii dii

cell phone 携帯電話 keetai denwa

Celsius 摂氏 sesshi

centimeter センチメートル senchi-meetoru

chair 椅子 isu

chair lift スキーリフト sukii rifuto

change v (buses) 乗り換えます norikaemasu; ~ v (money) 替えます kaemasu; ~ v (baby) おむつを替えます omutsu o kaemasu; ~ n (plan) 変更 henkoo; ~ n (money) お釣り otsuri

charcoal 炭 sumi

charge v (credit card) カードで払います kaado de haraimasu; n (cost) 料金 ryookin

cheap 安い yasui

cheaper もっと安い motto yasui

check v (something) 調べます shirabemasu; ~ v (luggage) 預けます azukemasu; ~ n (payment) お勘定 okanjoo

check-in チェックイン chekku in

checking account 当座預金口座 tooza yoking kooza

check-out (hotel) n チェックアウト chekku auto

chemical toilet ケミカルトイレ kemikaru toire

chemist [BE] 薬局 yakkyoku

cheque [BE] チェック chekku

chest (body part) 胸 mune

chest pain 胸の痛み mune no itami

chewing gum ガム gamu

child 子供 kodomo

child's seat 子供用の椅子 kodomoyoo no isu

children's menu 子供用のメニュー kodomoyoo no menyuu

children's portion 子供用のメニュー kodomoyoo no menyuu

china 瀬戸物 setomono

China 中国 chuugoku

Chinese 中国語 chuugokugo

chopsticks おはし ohashi

church 教会 kyookai

cigar 葉巻 hamaki

cigarette 煙草 tabako

class クラス kurasu

clay pot 土器 doki

classical music クラシック音楽 kurashikku ongaku

clean v きれいにします kirei ni shimasu; ~ adj きれい kiree

cleaning product 洗浄剤 senjoozai

cleaning supplies クリーニング用品 kuriiningu yoohin

clear v (on an ATM) 消去します shookyo shimasu

cliff 崖 gake

cling film [BE] ラップ rappu

close v (a shop) 閉めます shimemasu; ~ adj 近い chikai

closed 閉館 heekan

clothing 衣類 irui

clothing store 洋服屋 yoofukuya

club クラブ kurabu

coat コート kooto

coffee shop 喫茶店 kissaten

coin 硬貨 kooka

cold (sickness) 風邪 kaze; ~ (weather) 寒い samui; ~ (food) 冷たい tsumetai colleague 同僚 dooryoo

cologne オーデコロン oodekoron

color 色 iro

comb 櫛 kushi

come v 来ます kimasu

complaint 苦情 kujoo

computer コンピュータ konpyuuta

concert コンサート konsaato

concert hall コンサートホ
ール konsaato hooru

condition (medical) 症状 shoojoo

conditioner コンディショナー
kondishonaa

condom コンドーム kondoomu

conference 会議 kaigi

confirm v 確認します kakunin
shimasu

congestion 混雑 konzatsu

connect v (internet) 接続します
setsuzoku shimasu

connection (internet) 接続
setsuzoku; ~ (flight) 連絡 renraku

constipated 便秘 benpi

consulate 領事館 ryoojikan

consultant コンサルタント konsa-
rutanto

contact v 連絡します renraku
shimasu

contact lens コンタクトレンズ kontakuto renzu; ~ solution コンタクトレ
ンズ液 kontakuto renzu eki

contagious 伝染性 densensee

convention hall 会議場 kaigijoo

conveyor belt コンベヤーベルト
konbeyaa beruto

cook v 料理します ryoori shimasu

cooking gas ガス gasu

cool (temperature) 涼しい suzushii

copper 銅 doo

corkscrew コルクスクリュー koruku
sukuryuu

cost v かかります kakarimasu

cot 折り畳みベッド oritatami beddo

cotton 綿／コットン men/kotton

cough 咳 seki

country code 国番号 kuni bangoo

cover charge カバーチャ
ージ kabaa chaaji

crash v (car) ぶつかります butsukarimasu

cream (ointment) 軟膏 nankoo

credit card クレジットカード
kurejitto kaado

crew neck クルーネック kuruu nekku

crib ベビーベッド bebii beddo

crystal 水晶 suishoo

cup カップ kappu

currency 通貨 tsuuka

currency exchange 両替 ryoogae;
~ office 両替所 ryoogaejo

current account [BE] 当座預金
tooza yokin

customs 税関 zeekan

cut v (hair) カット katto

cut n (injury) 傷 kizu

cute 可愛い kawaii

cycling サイクリング saikuringu

D

damage v 壊れます kowaremasu

damaged 壊れた kowareta

dance v 踊ります odorimasu

dance club ダンスクラブ dansu kurabu

dangerous 危ない abunai

dark 暗い kurai

date (calendar) 日付け hizuke

day 日 hi

deaf 耳が聞こえない mimi ga kikoenai

debit card デビットカード debitto kaado

deck chair デッキチェア dekki chea

declare v 申告します shisnkoku shimasu

decline v (credit card) 拒否します kyohi shimasu

deeply 深く fukaku

degrees (temperature) 度 do

delay v 遅れます okuremasu

delete v 削除します sakujo shimasu

delicatessen デリカテッセン derikatessen

delicious おいしい oishii

denim デニム denimu

dentist 歯医者 haisha

denture 入れ歯 ireba

deodorant デオドラント deodoranto

department store デパート depaato

departure 出発 shuppatsu

deposit v 預けます azukemasu; ~ n (security) 前金 maekin

desert 砂漠 sabaku

detergent 洗剤 senzai

diabetic 糖尿病 toonyoobyoo

dial v 電話をかけます denwa o kakemasu

diamond ダイアモンド daiamondo

diaper おむつ omutsu

diarrhea 下痢 geri

diesel ディーゼル diizeru

difficult 難しい muzukashii

digital デジタル dejitaru; ~ camera デジタルカメラ dejitaru kamera; ~ photo デジタル写真 dejitaru shashin ~ print デジタルカメラプリント dejitaru kamera purinto

dining room 食堂 shokudoo

dinner 食事 shokuji

direction 方向 hookoo

dirty 汚い kitanai

disabled 身体障害者 shintai shoogai-sha; ~ accessible [BE] バリアフリー設備 baria furii setsubi

disconnect (computer) 接続を切ります setsuzoku o kirimasu

discount 割引 waribiki

dish (kitchen) 食器 shokki

dishwasher 皿洗い機 sara araiki

dishwashing liquid 中性洗剤 chuu-see senzai

display 表示 hyooji

display case ショーケース shookeesu

disposable 使い捨て tsukaisute

disposable razor 使い捨てカミソリ tsukaisute kamisori

dive V 飛び込みます tobikomimasu

diving equipment 潜水用具 sensui yoogu

divorce V 離婚します rikon shimasu

dizzy めまいがします memai ga shimasu

doctor 医者 isha

doll 人形 ningyoo

dollar (U.S.) ドル doru

domestic 国内の kokunai no

domestic flight 国内線 kokunaisen

dormitory 寮 ryoo

double bed ダブルベッド daburu beddo

downtown 繁華街 hankagai

dozen ダース daasu

drag lift 抗力浮揚 kooryoku fuyoo

dress (piece of clothing) ワンピース wanpiisu

dress code 服装規定 fukusoo kitee

drink V 飲みます nomimasu; ~ n 飲み物 nomimono

drink menu ドリンクメニュー dorinku menyuu

drinking water 飲料水 inryoosui

drive V 運転します unten shimasu

driver's license 運転免許証 unten menkyoshoo; ~ number 運転免許証番号 unten menkyoshoo bangoo

drop (medicine) 一滴 itteki

drowsiness 眠気 nemuke

dry cleaner ドライクリーニング店 dorai kuriiningu ten

during …の間 …no aida

duty (tax) 関税 kanzee

duty-free 免税 menzee

DVD DVD dii bui dii

E

ear 耳 mimi

earache 耳の痛み mimi no itami

early 早い hayai

earrings イヤリング iyaringu

east 東 higashi

easy やさしい yasashii

eat V 食べます tabeamasu

economy class エコノミークラス ekonomii kurasu

elbow 肘 hiji

electric outlet コンセント konsento

elevator エレベーター erebeetaa

e-mail V メールします meeru shimasu; ~ n 電子メール denshi meeru

e-mail address 電子メールアドレス denshi meeru adoresu

emergency 緊急 kinkyuu

emergency exit 非常口 hijoo guchi

empty V 空にします kara ni shimasu

end V 終わります owarimasu

English イギリス人 igirisujin; (language) 英語 eego

engrave V 彫り込みます horikomimasu

enjoy V 楽しみます tanoshimimasu

enter V 入ります hairimasu; (computer) 入力します nyuuryoku shimasu

entertainment エンターテインメント entaateenmento

entrance 入口 iriguchi

envelope 封筒 fuutoo

equipment 道具 doogu

escalator エスカレーター esuka-reetaa

e-ticket Eチケット i chiketto

evening 夕方 yuugata

excess 超過 chooka

exchange v (money) 両替します ryoogae shimasu; ~ v (goods) 取り替えます torikaemasu; ~ n (place) 交換所 kookanjo

exchange rate (為替)レート (kawase)reeto

excursion エクスカーション ekusu-kaashon

excuse v 許します yurushimasu

exhausted 疲れている tsukareteiru

exit v 出ます demasu; ~ n 出口 deguchi

expensive 高い takai

expert (skill level) 専門家 senmonka

exposure (film) ...枚撮り ...maitori

express (mail) 速達 sokutatsu; (train) 急行 kyuukoo

extension (phone) 内線 naisen

extra 特別な tokubetsuna

extra large 特大 tokudai

extract v (tooth) 抜きます nukimasu

eye 目 me

F

face 顔 kao

facial フェーシャル feesharu

family 家族 kazoku

fan (appliance) 扇風機 senpuuki

far 遠い tooi

far-sighted 遠視の enshi no

farm 農家 nooka

fast 速い hayai

fast food ファーストフード faasuto fuudo

fat free 無脂肪 mushiboo

father (one's own) 父 chichi; (someone else's) お父さん otoosan

fax v ファックスします fakkusu shimasu; ~ n ファックス fakkusu

fax number ファックス番号 fakkusu bangoo

fee 費用 hiyoo

feed v 授乳します junyuu shimasu

ferry フェリー ferii

fever 熱 netsu

field (sports) フィールド fiirudo

fill up v (food) 満タンにします mantan ni shimasu

fill out v (form) 記入します kinyuu shimasu

filling (tooth) 詰物 tsumemono

film (camera) フィルム fuirumu

fine (fee) 罰金 bakkin

finger 指 yubi

fingernail 爪 tsume

fire 火 hi

fire department 消防署 shooboosho

fire door 耐火扉 taika tobira

first 最初の saisho no

first class ファーストクラス faasuto kurasu

fish 魚 sakana

fit (clothing) 合います aimasu

fitting room 試着室 shichakushitsu

fix v (repair) 直します naoshi masu

flashlight 懐中電灯 kaichuu dentoo

flight 便 bin

floor 階 kai

flower 花 hana

folk music フォークミュージック
  fooku myuujikku

food 食物 tabemono

foot 足 ashi

football game [BE] サッカーゲーム
  sakkaa geemu

for (a day) 一日間 ichiinichiikan

forecast 予報 yohoo

foreigner 外国人 gaikokujin

forest 森 mori

fork フォーク fooku

form (fill-in) 用紙 yooshi

formula (baby) フォーミュラ
  foomyura

fountain 噴水 funsui

free (not busy) 暇 hima;
  ~ (available) 空いています aiteimasu;

free (no charge) 無料 muryoo

freezer 冷凍庫 reetooko

fresh 新しい atarashii

friend 友人 yuujin

frying pan フライパン furaipan

full-service 完全サービス kanzen
  saabisu

game ゲーム geemu

garage 修理工場 shuurikoojoo

garbage bag ごみ袋 gomibukuro

gas ガソリン gasorin

gas station ガソリンスタンド gasorin
  sutando

gate (airport) ゲート geeto

gay bar ゲイバー gei baa

gay club ゲイクラブ gei kurabu

gel (hair) ジェル jeru

get to 着きます tsukimasu

get off (a train/bus/subway)
  下ります orimasu

gift 贈り物 okurimono

gift shop 売店 baiten

girl 女の子 onna no ko

girlfriend ガールフレンド gaaru
  furendo

give v 上げます agemasu

glass (drinking) コップ koppu;
  ~ (material) ガラス garasu

glasses 眼鏡 megane

go v (somewhere) 行きます ikimasu

gold 金 kin

golf course ゴルフ場 gorufujoo

golf tournament ゴルフトーナメント
  gorufu toonamento

good 良い ii; (food) おいしい
  oishii

good afternoon 今日は konnichiwa

good evening 今晩は konbanwa

good morning お早うございます
  ohayoo gozaimasu

goodbye さようなら sayoonara

gram グラム guramu

grandchild 孫 mago

grandparent (one's own) 祖父/祖母 sofu/sobo; (someone else's) おじいさん／おばあさん ojiisan/obaasan

gray グレー guree

green 緑／グリーン midori/guriin

grocery store 食料品店 shokuryoohinten

ground floor 一階 ikkai

group グループ guruupu

guide n ガイド gaido

guide book ガイドブック gaido bukku

guide dog 盲導犬 moodoo ken

gym トレーニングジム toreeningu jimu

gynecologist 婦人科医 fujinkai

H

hair 髪 kami

hair dryer ヘアドライヤー hea doraiyaa

hair salon 美容院 biyooin

hairbrush ヘアブラシ hea burashi

haircut ヘアカット hea katto

hairspray ヘアスプレー hea supuree

hairstyle ヘアスタイル hea sutairu

hairstylist ヘアスタイリスト hea sutairisuto

half 半分 hanbun

half hour 半時間 han jikan

half-kilo 半キロ han kiro

hammer ハンマー hanmaa

hand 手 te

hand luggage [BE] 手荷物 tenimotsu

handbag [BE] ハンドバッグ hando baggu

handicapped 身体障害者 shintai shoogaisha

handicapped-accessible ハンディキャップ用 handikyappuyoo

hangover 二日酔い futsuka yoi

happy 楽しい tanoshii

hat 帽子 booshi

have v あります arimasu

head (body part) 頭 atama

headache 頭痛 zutsuu

headphones ヘッドフォン heddofon

health 健康 kenkoo

health food store 健康食品店 kenkoo shokuhinten

heart 心臓 shinzoo

heart condition 心臓病 shinzoobyoo

heat 熱 netsu

heater 暖房 danboo

heating [BE] ヒーター／暖房 hiitaa/danboo

hello 今日は konnichiwa; (on the phone) もしもし moshi moshi

helmet ヘルメット herumetto

help 助け tasuke

here ここ koko

hi どうも doomo

high 高い takai

highchair ハイチェアー haicheaa

highway ハイウェー haiuee

hill 丘 oka

hire v[BE] 借ります karimasu

hire car [BE] レンタルカー rentarukaa

hitchhike v ヒッチハイクします hitchi haiku shimasu

hockey ホッケー hokkee

holiday [BE] 休日 kyuujitsu

horse track 競馬場 keebajoo

hospital 病院 byooin

hostel ホステル hosuteru

hot (temperature) 暑い atsui;
~ (spicy) 辛い karai

hot spring 温泉 onsen

hot water お湯 oyu

hotel ホテル hoteru

hour 時間 jikan

house 家 ie

household good 家庭用品 katee yoohin

housekeeping services 客室清掃サービス kyakushitsu seesoo saabisu

how どうやって dooyatte

how much (money) いくら ikura;
(quantity) どのくらい dono kurai

hungry お腹がすいた onaka ga suita

hurt 痛い itai

husband (one's own) 主人 shujin;
(some one else's) ご主人 goshujin

I

ibuprofen イブプロフェン ibuprofen

ice 氷 koori

ice hockey アイスホッケー aisu hokkee

icy 氷の koori no

identification 身分証明 mibun shoomee

ill 病気 byooki

include v 含みます fukumimasu

indoor pool 室内プール shitsunai puuru

inexpensive 安い yasui

infected 感染した kansen shita

information (phone) 案内 annai

information desk 受付 uketsuke

inn 旅館 ryokan

insect bite 虫さされ mushi sasare

insect repellent 虫除け mushi yoke

insert v (on an ATM) 挿入します／入れます soonyuu shimasu/iremasu

insomnia 不眠症 fuminshoo

instant message インスタント・メッセージ insutanto messeeji

insulin インスリン insurin

insurance 保険 hoken; v 保険を掛けます hoken o kakemasu

insurance card 保険証 hokenshoo

insurance company 保険会社 hoken gaisha

interesting 面白い omoshiroi

international (airport area) 国際 kokusai

international flight 国際線 kokusaisen

international student card 留学生証 ryuugakuseeshoo

internet インターネット intaanetto

internet cafe インターネットカフェ intaanetto kafe

internet service インターネットサービス intaanetto saabisu

interpreter 通訳者 tsuuyakusha

intersection 交差点 koosaten

intestine 腸 choo

introduce V 紹介します shookai shimasu

invoice 請求書 seekyuusho

Ireland アイルランド airurando

Irish アイルランド人 airurando jin

iron V アイロンをかけます airon o kakemasu; ~ n アイロン airon

J

jacket ジャケット jaketto

Japanese (people) 日本人 nihonjin

Japanese (language) 日本語 nihongo

jar 瓶 bin

jaw 顎 ago

jazz ジャズ jazu

jazz club ジャズクラブ jazu kurabu

jeans ジーパン／ジーンズ jiipan/jiinzu

jeweler 宝石店 hoosekiten

jewelry 宝石 hooseki

join V 加入します kanyuu shimasu

joint (body part) 関節 kansetsu

K

key 鍵 kagi

key card 鍵カード kagi kaado

key ring キーホルダー kii horudaa

kiddie pool 子供用プール kodomoyoo puuru

kidney (body part) 腎臓 jinzoo

kilogram キロ(グラム) kiro(guramu)

kilometer キロ(メートル) kiro(meetoru)

kiss V キスします kisu shimasu

kitchen 台所 daidokoro; ~ foil [BE] アルミフォイル arumifoiru

knee 膝 hiza

knife ナイフ naifu

L

lace レース reesu

lacquerware 漆器 shikki

lactose intolerant 乳糖不耐症 nyuutoo futaishoo

lake 湖 mizuumi

large 大きい ookii

last 最後 saigo

late (time) 遅い osoi

later あとで atode

launderette [BE] コインランドリー koin randorii

laundromat コインランドリー koin randorii

laundry 洗濯 sentaku

laundry facility 洗濯施設 sentaku shisetsu

laundry service ランドリーサービス randorii saabisu

lawyer 弁護士 bengoshi

leather 皮 kawa

leave v 出ます demasu

left (direction) 左 hidari

leg 脚 ashi

lens レンズ renzu

less もっと少ない motto sukunai

lesson レッスン ressun

letter 手紙 tegami

library 図書館 toshokan

life boat 救命ボート kyuumee booto

life jacket 救命胴衣 kyuumee dooi

lifeguard ライフガード raifu gaado

lift リフト rifuto; ~ [BE] エレベータ
ー erebeetaa

lift pass adj リフト券 rifuto ken

light (overhead) 電灯 dentoo;
~ v (cigarette) 火をつけます
hi o tsukemasu

lightbulb 電球 denkyuu

lighter ライター raitaa

like v 好きです sukidesu

line (train) 線 sen

linen 麻 asa

lip 唇 kuchibiru

liquor store 酒屋 sakaya

liter リットル rittoru

little 少し／ちょっと
sukoshi/chotto

live v 住みます sumimasu

liver (body part) 肝臓 kanzoo

loafers ローファー roofaa

local 地方 chihoo

lock v 鍵をかけます kagi o
kakemasu; ~ n 鍵 kagi

locker ロッカー rokkaa

log on ログオンします roggu on
shimasu

log off ログオフします roggu ofu
shimasu

long 長い nagai

long sleeves 長袖 nagasode

long-sighted [BE] 遠視 enshi

look v 見ます mimasu

lose v (something) なくします
nakushimasu

lost 道に迷いました michi ni mayoi
mashita

lost and found お忘れ物承り所
owasure mono uketamawari jo

lotion ローション rooshon

louder もっと大きい声で motto ookii
koe de

love 愛 ai

low 低い hikui

luggage 荷物 nimotsu

luggage cart カート kaato

luggage locker コインロッカー koin
rokkaa

luggage ticket 荷物引換券 nimotsu
hikikae ken

lunch 昼食 chuushoku

lung 肺 hai

M

magazine 雑誌 zasshi

magnificent 立派 rippa

mail v 郵送します yuusoo
shimasu; ~ n 手紙 tegami

mailbox 郵便ポスト yuubin posuto

main attraction メインイベント mein ibento

main course メインコース mein koosu

make up a prescription [BE] 調合します choogoo shimasu

mall ショッピングモール shoppingu mooru

man 男の人 otoko no hito

manager (restaurant, hotel) 支配人 shihainin; **(shop)** 店長 tenchoo

manicure マニキュア manikyua

manual car マニュアル manyuaru

map n 地図 chizu

market マーケット maaketto

married 結婚している kekkon shiteiru

marry v 結婚します kekkon shimasu

mass (church service) ミサ misa

massage マッサージ massaaji

match n 試合 shiai

meal 食事 shokuji

measure v **(someone)** 測ります hakarimasu

measuring cup 計量カップ keeryoo kappu

measuring spoon 計量スプーン keeryoo supuun

mechanic 修理工 shuurikoo

medicine 薬 kusuri

medium (size) 中ぐらい chuugurai

meet v **(someone)** 待ち合わせます machiawasemasu

meeting 会議 kaigi

meeting room 会議室 kaigishitsu

membership card 会員証 kaiin shoo

memorial (place) 記念館 kinenkan

memory card メモリーカード memorii kaado

mend v 直します naoshimasu

menstrual cramp 生理痛 seiritsuu

menu メニュー menyuu

message メッセージ, ご伝言 messeeji, godengon

meter (parking) 料金メーター ryookin meetaa

microwave 電子レンジ denshi renji

midday [BE] 昼間 hiruma

midnight 真夜中 mayonaka

mileage 距離 kyori

mini-bar ミニバー mini baa

minute 分 fun/pun

missing いなくなる inakunaru

mistake 間違い machigai

mobile phone [BE] 携帯電話 keetai denwa

mobility 移動性 idoosee

money お金 okane

month 月 tsuki

mop モップ moppu

moped モペット mopetto

more もっと motto

morning 朝 asa

mosque 回教寺院 kaikyoo jiin

mother (one's own) 母 haha; **(someone else's)** お母さん okaasan

motion sickness 乗物酔い norimono yoi

motor boat モーターボート mootaa booto

motorcycle オートバイ ootobai

motorway [BE] 高速道路 koosoku dooro

mountain 山 yama

mountain bike マウンテンバイク maunten baiku

mousse (hair) ムース muusu

mouth 口 kuchi

movie 映画 eega

movie theater 映画館 eegakan

mug V襲います osoimasu

muscle 筋肉 kinniku

museum 博物館 hakubutsukan

music 音楽 ongaku

music store 楽器屋 gakkiya

N

nail file ネイルファイル neeru fairu

nail salon ネイルサロン neeru saron

name 名前 namae

napkin ナプキン napukin

nappy [BE] おむつ omutsu

nationality 国籍 kokuseki

nature preserve 自然保護区 shizen hogoku

nauseous 吐き気 hakike

near 近く chikaku

near-sighted 近視 kinshi

nearby 近く chikaku

neck 首 kubi

necklace ネックレス nekkuresu

need V要ります irimasu

newspaper 新聞 shinbun

newsstand キオスク kiosuku

next 次 tsugi

nice すてき suteki

night 夜 yoru

nightclub ナイトクラブ naito kurabu

no いいえ iie

non-alcoholic ノンアルコール non arukooru

non-smoking 禁煙 kin-en

noon 正午 shoogo

north 北 kita

nose 鼻 hana

note [BE] お札 osatsu

notify V知らせます shirasemasu

novice (skill level) 初心者 shoshin-sha

now 今 ima

number 数字 suuji

nurse 看護士 kangoshi

O

office オフィス ofisu

office hours オフィスアワー ofisu awaa

off-licence [BE] 酒屋 sakaya

oil オイル oiru

OK オーケー ookee

old (person) 年寄り toshiyori; (thing) 古い furui

on the corner 角の kadono

once 一度 ichido

one 一つ hitotsu

one-way (ticket) 片道 katamichi

one-way street 一方通行 ippoo tsuukoo

only ただ tada
open v 開けます akemasu;
~ *adj* 開いている aiteiru
opera オペラ opera
opera house オペラハウス opera
hausu
opposite 向かい mukai
optician 眼鏡店 meganeten
orange (color) オレンジ色 orenji iro
orchestra オーケストラ ookesutora
order v 注文します chuumon
shimasu
outdoor pool 屋外プール okugai
puuru
outside 外 soto
over the counter (medication)
処方箋無し shohoosen nashi
overdone 焼き過ぎ yakisugi
overlook (scenic place) 見晴し台
miharashidai
overnight 夜通し yodooshi
oxygen treatment 酸素治療 sanso
chiryoo

P

p.m. *n* 午後 gogo (1 p.m.; gogo ichiji)
pacifier おしゃぶり oshaburi
pack v 詰めます tsumemasu
package 小包 kozutsumi
paddling pool [BE] 子供用プール
kodomoyoo puuru
pad [BE] 生理用ナプキン
seeriyoo napukin
pain 痛み itami
pajamas パジャマ pajama

palace 宮殿 kyuuden
pants ズボン zubon
pantyhose パンスト pansuto
paper 紙 kami
paper towel ペーパータオル peepaa
taoru
paracetamol [BE] アセタミノーフェ
ン asetaminoofen
park v 駐車します chuusha shimasu;
~ *n* 公園 kooen
parking garage 駐車場 chuushajoo
parking lot 駐車場 chuushajoo
parking meter 料金メーター ryookin
meetaa
part (for car) 部品 buhin
part-time パートタイム paato taimu
passenger 乗客 jookyaku
passport パスポート pasupooto
passport control 入国手続き nyuukoku tetsuzuki
password パスワード pasu waado
pastry shop ケーキ屋 keekiya
path 道路 dooro
pay v 払います haraimasu
pay phone 公衆電話 kooshuu denwa
peak (of a mountain) 山頂 sanchoo
pearl 真珠 shinju
pedestrian 歩行者 hokoosha
pediatrician 小児科医 shoonikai
pedicure ペディキュア pedikyua
pen ペン pen
penicillin ペニシリン penishirin
penis ペニス penisu
per につき nitsuki
per day 一日につき ichinichi ni tsuki

per hour 一時間につき ichijikan ni tsuki

per night 一晩につき hitoban ni tsuki

per week 一週間につき isshuukan ni tsuki

perfume 香水 koosui

period (menstrual) 生理 seeri; ~(of time) 期間 kikan

permit v 許可します kyoka shimasu

petite ペティート petiito

petrol [BE] ガソリン gasorin

petrol station [BE] ガソリンスタンド gasorin sutando

pharmacy 薬局 yakkyoku

phone v 電話します denwa shimasu; ~ n 電話 denwa

phone call 電話 denwa

phone card テレホンカード terehon kaado

phone number 電話番号 denwa bangoo

photo 写真 shashin

photocopy コピー kopii

photography 写真撮影 shashin satsuee

pick up (something) 受け取ります uketorimasu

picnic area ピクニック場 pikunik-kujoo

pill (birth control) ピル piru

pillow 枕 makura

personal identification number (PIN) 暗証番号 anshoo bangoo

pink ピンク pinku

piste [BE] ゲレンデ gerende

piste map [BE] ゲレンデ地図 gerende chizu

pizzeria ピザ・レストラン piza resutoran

place v (a bet) 掛け金を払います kakekin o haraimasu; n 場所 basho

plane 飛行機 hikooki

plastic wrap ラップ rappu

plate 皿 sara

platform ホーム hoomu

platinum プラチナ purachina

play v します shimasu; ~ n (theatre) 芝居 shibai

playground 公園 kooen

playpen ベビーサークル bebii saakuru

please (asking for a favor) お願いします onegai shimasu; (offering a favor) どうぞ doozo

pleasure 楽しみ tanoshimi

plunger トイレの吸引具 toire no kyuuingu

plus size プラスサイズ purasu saizu

pocket ポケット poketto

poison 毒 doku

poles (skiing) ストック sutokku

police 警察 keesatsu

police report 警察の証明書 keesatsu no shoomeesho

police station 交番 kooban

pond 池 ike

pool プール puuru

pop music ポピュラー音楽 popyuraa ongaku

portion 部分 bubun

post [BE] 手紙 tegami

post office 郵便局 yuubinkyoku

postbox [BE] 郵便ポスト yuubin posuto

postcard 葉書 hagaki

pot 深鍋 fukanabe

pottery 陶器 tooki

pound (weight) ポンド pondo; ~ (British sterling) ポンド pondo

pregnant 妊娠 ninshin

prepaid phone プリペイド 携帯 puripeedo keetai

prescribe V 処方します shohoo shimasu

prescription 処方箋 shohoosen

press V (clothing) アイロンをかけます airon o kakemasu

price 値段 nedan

print V 印刷します insatsu shimasu

problem 問題 mondai

produce 食料品 shokuryoohin

produce store 食料品店 shokuryoohinten

prohibit V 禁止します kinshi shimasu

pronounce V 発音します hatsuon shimasu

public 公共 kookyoo

pull V 引きます hikimasu

purple 紫 murasaki

purse 財布 saifu

push V 押します oshimasu

pushchair [BE] ベビーカー bebii kaa

Q

quality 質 shitsu

question 質問 shitsumon

quiet 静か shizuka

R

racetrack 競馬場 keebajoo

racket (sports) ラケット raketto

railway station [BE] 駅 eki

rain n 雨 ame

raincoat レインコート reinkooto

rainforest 雨林 urin

rainy 雨の ameno

rap (music) ラップ rappu

rape 強姦 gookan

rash 発疹 hasshin

razor blade カミソリの刃 kamisori no ha

reach V 届きます todokimasu

ready 用意ができている yooi ga dekite iru

real 本物 honmono

receipt レシート／領収書 reshiito/ryooshuusho

receive V 受け取ります uketorimasu

reception 受付 uketsuke

recharge V 充電します juuden shimasu

recommend V 推薦します suisen shimasu

recommendation 推薦 suisen

recycling リサイクリング risaikuringu

red 赤い akai

refrigerator 冷蔵庫 reezooko

region 地域 chiiki

registered mail 書留 kakitome

regular レギュラー regyuraa

relationship 関係 kankee

rent *V* 借ります karimasu

rental car レンタカー rentakaa

repair *V* 修理します shuuri shimasu

repeat *V* もう一度言います moo ichido iimasu

reservation 予約 yoyaku

reservation desk 予約窓口 yoyaku madoguchi

reserve *V* 予約します yoyaku shimasu

restaurant レストラン resutoran

restroom 化粧室 keshooshitsu

retired 退職した taishoku shita

return *V* 返します kaeshimasu; ~ *n* [BE] 往復 oofuku

rib (body part) 肋骨 rokkotsu

rice cooker 炊飯器 suihanki

right (direction) 右 migi

right of way 優先権 yuusenken

ring 指輪／リング yubiwa/ringu

river 川 kawa

road map 道路地図 dooro chizu

rob *V* 盗みます nusumimasu

robbed 盗まれました nusumare mashita

romantic ロマンチック romanchikku

room 部屋 heya

room key 部屋の鍵 heya no kagi

room service ルームサービス ruumu saabisu

round-trip 往復 oofuku

route コース koosu

rowboat ボート booto

rubbish [BE] ゴミ gomi

rubbish bag [BE] ゴミ袋 gomi bukuro

ruins 遺跡 iseki

rush ラッシュ rasshu

S

sad 悲しい kanashii

safe (thing) 金庫 kinko; ~ **(protected)** 安全 anzen

sales tax 消費税 shoohizee

sandals サンダル sandaru

sanitary napkin 生理用ナプキン seeriyoo napukin

saucepan 鍋 nabe

sauna サウナ sauna

save *V* **(on a computer)** 保存します hozon shimasu

savings (account) 普通預金 futsuu yokin

scanner スキャナー sukyanaa

scarf スカーフ sukaafu

schedule *V* 予定に入れます yotee ni iremasu; ~ *n* 予定 yotee

school 学校 gakkoo

science 科学 kagaku

scissors はさみ hasami

sea 海 umi

seat 席 seki

security 警備 keebi

see *V* 見ます mimasu

self-service セルフサービス serufu saabisu

sell *V* 売ります urimasu

seminar セミナー seminaa

send *V* 送ります okurimasu

senior citizen 高齢者 kooreesha

separated (marriage) 別居 bekkyo

serious 真面目な majimena

service (in a restaurant) サービス saabisu

sexually transmitted disease (STD) 性病 seebyoo

shampoo シャンプー shanpuu

sharp 鋭い surudoi

shaving cream シェービングクリーム sheebingu kuriimu

sheet シーツ shiitsu

ship *V* (mail) 送ります okurimasu

shirt シャツ shatsu

shoe store 靴屋 kutsuya

shoes 靴 kutsu

shop *V* 買い物をします kaimono o shimasu

shopping 買い物 kaimono

shopping area 商店街 shooten gai

shopping centre [BE] ショッピングセンター shoppingu sentaa

shopping mall ショッピングモール shoppingu mooru

short 短い mijikai

short sleeves 半袖 hansode

shorts 半ズボン hanzubon

short-sighted [BE] 近視 kinshi

shoulder 肩 kata

show *V* 見せます misemasu

shower シャワー shawaa

shrine 神社 jinja

sick 病気 byooki

side dish 付け合わせ tsukeawase

side effect 副作用 fukusayoo

sightseeing 観光 kankoo

sightseeing tour 観光ツアー kankoo tsuaa

sign *V* 署名します／サインします shomeeshimasu/sainshimasu

silk 絹 kinu

silver 銀 gin

single (unmarried) 独身 dokushin

single bed シングルベッド shinguru beddo

single room シングルルーム shinguru ruumu

sink 流し nagashi

sister (my older) 姉 ane

sister (my younger) 妹 imooto

sister (someone else's older) お姉さん oneesan

sister (someone else's younger) 妹さん imootosan

sit *V* 座ります suwarimasu

size サイズ saizu

skin 皮膚 hifu

skirt スカート sukaato

ski スキー sukii

ski lift スキーリフト sukii rifuto

sleep *V* 眠ります nemurimasu

sleeper car 寝台車 shindaisha

sleeping bag 寝袋／スリーピングバッグ nebukuro/suriipingu baggu

slice (of something) 一切れ hitokire

slippers スリッパ surippa

slower もっとゆっくり motto yukkuri

slowly ゆっくり yukkuri

small 小さい chiisai

smaller もっと小さい motto chiisai

smoke V煙草を吸います tabako o suimasu

smoking (area) 喫煙席 kitsuenseki

snack bar スナックバー sunakku baa

sneaker スニーカー suniikaa

snorkeling equipment スノーケル用具 sunookeru yoogu

snowboard スノーボード sunoo boodo

snowshoe 雪靴 yukigutsu

snowy 雪の多い yuki no ooi

soap 石鹸 sekken

soccer サッカー sakkaa

sock 靴下 kutsushita

soother [BE] おしゃぶり oshaburi

sore throat 喉の痛み nodo no itami

sorry ごめんなさい gomennasai

south 南 minami

souvenir お土産 omiyage

souvenir store お土産屋 omiyageya

spa 温泉 onsen

spatula へら hera

speak V話します hanashimasu

specialist (doctor) 専門医 senmon-i

specimen 見本 mihon

speeding スピード違反 supiido ihan

spell V つづりを言います tsuzuri o iimasu

spicy 辛い karai

spine (body part) 脊椎 sekitsui

spoon スプーン supuun

sports スポーツ supootsu

sporting goods store スポーツ用品店 supootsu yoohinten

sprain 捻挫 nenza

stadium スタジアム sutajiamu

stairs 階段 kaidan

stamp n (postage) 切手 kitte

start V (a car) スタートします sutaato shimasu

starter [BE] 前菜 zensai

station 駅 eki

statue 銅像 doozoo

stay V泊まります tomarimasu

steal V盗みます nusumimasu

steep 急斜面 kyuushamen

sterling silver 純銀 jungin

sting n虫さされ mushi sasare

stolen 盗まれた nusumareta

stomach 胃 i

stomachache 腹痛 fukutsuu

stop V止まります tomarimasu; ~ (bus) nバス停 basu tee

store directory 店内の案内 tennai no annai

storey [BE] 階 kai

stove コンロ konro

straight 真っ直ぐ massugu

strange 変 hen

stream 小川 ogawa

…Street …通り …doori

stroller 乳母車 ubaguruma

student 学生 gakusee

study V勉強します benkyoo shimasu

stunning 驚くほどの odoroku hodono

subtitle (movie) 字幕 jimaku

subway 地下鉄 chikatetsu

subway station 地下鉄の駅 chika-tetsu no eki

suit スーツ suutsu

suitcase スーツケース suutsu keesu

sun 太陽 taiyoo

sunblock 日焼け止めクリーム hiyake-dome kuriimu

sunburn 日焼け hiyake

sunglasses サングラス sangurasu

sunny 晴れの hareno

sunscreen 日除け hiyoke

sunstroke 日射病 nisshabyoo

super (fuel) スーパー suupaa

supermarket スーパー suupaa

surfboard サーフボード saafu boodo

sushi restaurant 寿司屋 sushi ya

swallow v 呑み込みます nomikomimasu

sweater セーター seetaa

sweatshirt トレーナー toreenaa

sweet (taste) 甘い amai

sweets [BE] キャンデー kyandee

swelling 腫れ hare

swim v 泳ぎます oyogimasu

swimsuit 水着 mizugi

symbol (keyboard) 記号 kigoo

synagogue ユダヤ教会 yudaya kyookai

T

table テーブル teeburu

tablet (medicine) 錠 joo

take v (medicine) 飲みます nomimasu

take away [BE] テークアウト teeku auto

tampon タンポン tanpon

taste v 味がします aji ga shimasu

taxi タクシー takushii

tea お茶 ocha

team チーム chiimu

teahouse 喫茶店 kissaten

teaspoon 茶匙 chasaji

telephone 電話 denwa

temple (religious) お寺 otera; **~ accommodation** 宿坊 shukuboo

temporary 一時的 ichijiteki

tennis テニス tenisu

tent テント tento

tent peg テント用ペグ tento yoo pegu

tent pole テントの支柱 tento no shichuu

terminal (airport) ターミナル taaminaru

terracotta テラコッタ terakotta

terrible ひどい hidoi

text v (send a message) メールを送ります meeru o okurimasu; ~ n (message) メール meeru

thank v 感謝します kansha shimasu

thank you ありがとう arigatoo

thank you (for food) ごちそうさまでした gochisoo sama deshita

that あれ are

theater 劇場 gekijoo

theft 盗難 toonan

there そこ soko

thief 泥棒 doroboo

thigh 腿 momo

thirsty 喉が渇きました nodo ga kawaki mashita

this これ kore

throat 喉 nodo

ticket 切符 kippu

ticket office 切符売り場 kippu uriba

tie (clothing) ネクタイ nekutai

time 時間 jikan

timetable [BE] 時刻表 jikokuhyoo

tire タイヤ taiya

tired 疲れました tsukare mashita

tissue ティッシュペーパー tisshu peepaa

tobacconist 煙草屋 tabakoya

today 今日 kyoo

toe 足指 ashi yubi

toenail 足の爪 ashi no tsume

toilet [BE] 化粧室 keshooshitsu

toilet paper トイレットペーパー toiretto peepaa

tomorrow あした ashita

tongue 舌 shita

tonight 今晩 konban

too …過ぎます …sugimasu

tooth 歯 ha

toothpaste 歯磨き粉 hamigakiko

total (amount) 合計 gookee

tough (food) 硬い katai

tourist 観光客 kankookyaku

tourist information office 観光案内所 kankoo annaijo

tour ツアー tsuaa

tow truck レッカー車 rekkaasha

towel タオル taoru

tower 塔 too

town 町 machi

town hall 市役所 shiyakusho

town map 市街地図 shigai chizu

town square 町の広場 machi no hiroba

toy 玩具 omocha

toy store 玩具屋 omochaya

track (train) 路線 rosen

traditional 伝統的 dentooteki

traffic light 信号 shingoo

trail 道 michi

trail map ハイキングコース案内 haikingu koosu annai

train 列車 ressha; (commuter train) 電車 densha

train station 駅 eki

transfer v (change trains/flights) 乗り換えます norikae masu; ~ v (money) 送金します sookin shimasu

translate v 翻訳します hon-yaku shimasu

trash ゴミ gomi

travel agency 旅行代理店 ryokoo dairiten

travel sickness 乗物酔い norimono yoi

traveler's check トラベラーズチェック toraberaazu chekku

traveller's cheque [BE] トラベラーズチェック toraberaazu chekku

tree 木 ki

trim v (hair) そろえます soroemasu

trip 旅行 ryokoo
trolley [BE] カート kaato
trousers [BE] ズボン zubon
T-shirt Tシャツ tii shatsu
turn off (lights) 消します keshimasu
turn on (lights) つけます tsukemasu
TV テレビ terebi
type V タイプします taipu shimasu
tyre [BE] タイヤ taiya

U

United Kingdom (U.K.) イギリス igirisu
United States (U.S.) アメリカ amerika
ugly みにくい minikui
umbrella 傘 kasa
unattended 無人の mujinno
unconscious 意識不明の ishiki fumeino
underground [BE] 地下鉄 chikatetsu
underground station [BE] 地下鉄の 駅 chikatetsu no eki
underpants [BE] パンツ pantsu
understand V 分かります wakari masu
underwear 下着 shitagi
university 大学 daigaku
unleaded (gas) 無鉛 muen
upper 上の ueno
urgent 緊急 kinkyuu
use V 使います／利用します tsukai masu/riyoo shimasu
username ユーザー名 yuuzaa mee
utensil 器具 kigu

V

vacancy 空き室 akishitsu
vacation 休假 kyuuka
vaccination 予防接種 yoboo sesshu
vacuum cleaner 電気掃除機 denki soojiki
vagina 膣 chitsu
vaginal infection 膣炎 chitsuen
valid 有効 yuukoo
valley 谷間 tanima
valuable 貴重な kichoona
value 値段 nedan
vegetarian ベジタリアン bejitarian
vehicle registration 自動車登録証 jidoosha toorokushoo
viewpoint [BE] 展望台 tenboodai
village 村 mura
vineyard ぶどう園 budooen
visa ビザ biza
visit V 訪れます otozure masu
visiting hours 開館時間 kaikan jikan
visually impaired 視覚障害者 shikaku shoogaisha
vitamin ビタミン bitamin
V-neck ネック V V nekku
volleyball game バレーボール試合 bareebooru shiai
vomit V 吐きます hakimasu

W

wait V 待ちます machimasu; ~ *n* 待ち時間 machi jikan
waiter ウェーター ueetaa

waiting room 待合室 machiaishitsu

waitress ウェートレス ueetoresu

wake v 起こします okoshi masu

wake-up call モーニングコール mooningu kooru

walk v 歩きます aruki masu; ~ n 散歩 sanpo

walking route 散歩道 sanpomichi

wall clock 柱時計 hashira dokee

wallet 財布 saifu

warm v (something) 暖めます atatame masu; ~ adj (temperature) 暖かい atatakai

washing machine 洗濯機 sentakuki

watch 腕時計 ude dokee

water 水 mizu

water skis 水上スキー suijoo sukii

waterfall 滝 taki

weather 天気 tenki

week 週 shuu

weekend 週末 shuumatsu

weekly 毎週 maishuu

welcome v 歓迎します kangei shimasu

well-rested よく休みました yoku yasumi mashita

west 西 nishi

what 何 nani

wheelchair 車椅子 kuruma isu

wheelchair ramp 車椅子用スロープ kuruma isu yoo suroopu

when いつ itsu

where どこ doko

white 白い shiroi

who 誰 dare

widowed 夫と死別した otto to shibetsu shita

wife (one's own) 家内 kanai; (someone else's) 奥さん okusan

window 窓 mado; ~ (on flight) 窓側 madogawa; **by the** ~ 窓際 madogiwa

wine list ワインリスト wain risuto

winter 冬 fuyu

wireless internet ワイアレスインターネット waiaresu intaanetto

wireless internet service ワイアレスインターネットサービス waiaresu intaanetto saabisu

wireless phone 携帯電話 keetai denwa

with (attached) …付き tsuki; (included) … 込み komi

withdraw v 引き出します hikidashi masu

withdrawal (bank) 引き出し hikidashi

without 無しで nashide

woman 女性 josee

wool ウール uuru

work v 働きます hataraki masu

wrap v (a package) 包みます tsutsumi masu

wrist 手首 tekubi

write v 書きます kaki masu

Y

year 年 toshi

yellow 黄色 kiiro

yen 円 en
yes はい hai
yesterday 昨日 kinoo
young 若い wakai
you're welcome どういたしまして doo itashi mashite

youth hostel ユースホステル yuusu hosuteru

Z

zero ゼロ／零 zero/ree
zoo 動物園 doobutsuen

Japanese–English Dictionary

A

aakeedo アーケード arcade

abunai 危ない dangerous

adaputa アダプタ adapter

afutaa sheebu アフターシェーブ aftershave

agemasu 上げます *v* give

ago 顎 jaw

ai 愛 love

aida 間 during

aimasu 合います fit (clothing)

airon アイロン iron

airon o kakemasu アイロンをかけます *v* iron (clothing)

airurando アイルランド Ireland

airurando jin アイルランド人 Irish

aisu hokkee アイスホッケー ice hockey

aiteimasu 空いています free (available)

aiteiru 開いている *adj* open

aji ga shimasu 味がします *v* taste

aji ga usui 味が薄い bland

ajia no アジアの Asian

akai 赤い red

akachan 赤ちゃん baby

akari 明かり light (overhead)

akemasu 開けます *v* open

akishitsu 空き室 vacancy

akusesarii アクセサリー accessories

akusesu shimasu アクセスします *v* access (Internet)

amai 甘い sweet (taste)

ame 雨 rain

ameno 雨の rainy

amerika no アメリカの American

amerika アメリカ United States (U.S.)

ane 姉 sister (my older)

ani 兄 brother (my older)

annai 案内 information (phone)

anshoo bangoo 暗証番号 personal identification number (PIN)

anzen 安全 safe (protected)

are あれ that

arerugii hannoo アレルギー反応 allergic reaction

arerugii アレルギー allergic

arigatoo ありがとう thank you

arimasu あります *v* have

aroma serapii アロマセラピー aromatherapy

aruki masu 歩きます *v* walk

arumi hoiru アルミホイル aluminum foil

asa 朝 morning

asa 麻 linen

asetaminoofen アセタミノーフェン paracetamol [BE]

ashi no tsume 足の爪 toenail

ashi 脚 leg

ashi 足 foot

ashikubi 足首 ankle

ashita あした tomorrow

atama 頭 head (body part)

atarashii 新しい fresh

atatakai 暖かい *adj* warm (temperature)

atatame masu 暖めます *v* warm (something)

ato 後 after

atode あとで later

atorakushon アトラクション attraction (place)

atsui 暑い hot (temperature)

azukemasu 預けます *v* deposit (money); check (luggage)

B

baa バー bar (place)

baggu バッグ bag

baiten 売店 gift shop

bakkin 罰金 fine (fee)

baree バレエ ballet

bareebooru shiai バレーボール試合 volleyball game

baria furii setsubi バリアフリー設備 disabled accessible [BE]

basho 場所 *n* place

basu バス bus

basu no kippu バスの切符 bus ticket

basu ryokoo バス旅行 bus tour

basu taaminaru バスターミナル bus station

basu teeryuujo バス停留所 bus stop

basuketto booru バスケットボール basketball

basutee バス停 bus stop

bebii beddo ベビーベッド crib

bebii kaa ベビーカー pushchair [BE]

bebii saakuru ベビーサークル playpen

bebii shittaa ベビーシッター babysitter

beddo ベッド bed

beeju ベージュ beige

bejitarian ベジタリアン vegetarian

bekkyo 別居 separated (marriage)

bengoshi 弁護士 lawyer

benjo 便所 restroom (informal)/ toilet [BE] (informal)

benkyoo shimasu 勉強します *v* study

benpi 便秘 constipated

beruto ベルト belt

biichi ビーチ beach

bijinesu kurasu ビジネス・クラス business class

bijinesu sentaa ビジネス・センター business center

bikini ビキニ bikini

bin 便 flight

bin 瓶 jar

biru ビル building

bitamin ビタミン vitamin

biyooin 美容院 hair salon

biza ビザ visa

boku 僕 I (male, informal)

bonyuu o agemasu 母乳をあげます breastfeed

booi furendo ボーイフレンド boyfriend

bookoo 膀胱 bladder

booru ボール bowl

booshi 帽子 hat
booto ボート rowboat
bubun 部分 portion
budooen ぶどう園 vineyard
buhin 部品 part (for car)
bui nekku ブイネック V-neck
burajaa ブラジャー bra
burausu ブラウス blouse
bureeki ブレーキ brakes (car)
buresuretto ブレスレット bracelet
buriifu ブリーフ briefs
buroochi ブローチ brooch
buruu ブルー blue
butsukarimasu ぶつかります
  v crash (car)
buutsu ブーツ boots
byooin 病院 hospital
byooki 病気 sick

C

chairo 茶色 brown
chairudo shiito チャイルドシート
  car seat
chasaji 茶匙 teaspoon
chekku チェック check
chekku auto チェックアウト
  check-out (hotel)
chekku in チェックイン check-in
chibusa 乳房 breast
chichi 父 father (one's own)
chihoo 地方 local
chiiki 地域 region
chiimu チーム team
chiisai 小さい small

chikai 近い close
chikaku 近く nearby
chikatetsu 地下鉄 subway/
  underground [BE]
chikatetsu no eki 地下鉄の駅
  subway station/underground [BE]
  station
chitsu 膣 vagina
chitsuen 膣炎 vaginal infection
chizu 地図 n map
choo 腸 intestine
choogoo shimasu 調合します
  v fill/make up [BE] (a prescription)
chooka 超過 excess
chooshoku 朝食 breakfast
chotto ちょっと little
chuugurai 中ぐらい medium (size)
chuumon shimasu 注文します
  v order
chuusee senzai 中性洗剤
  dishwashing liquid
chuusha shimasu 駐車します v park
chuushajoo 駐車場 parking
  garage/car park [BE]
chuushoku 昼食 lunch

D

daasu ダース dozen
daburu beddo ダブルベッド
  double bed
daiamondo ダイアモンド diamond
daidokoro 台所 kitchen
daigaku 大学 university
dainingu ruumu ダイニングルーム
  dining room

dairiten 代理店 agency

daiseedoo 大聖堂 cathedral

danboo 暖房 heater/heating [BE]

dansu kurabu ダンスクラブ dance club

dare 誰 who

debitto kaado デビットカード debit card

deguchi 出口 exit

dejitaru デジタル digital

dejitaru kamera デジタルカメラ digital camera

dejitaru kamera purinto デジタルカメラプリント digital print

dejitaru shashin デジタル写真 digital photo

dekki chea デッキチェア deck chair

demasu 出ます v leave

denchi 電池 battery

denimu デニム denim

denki soojiki 電気掃除機 vacuum cleaner

denkyuu 電球 lightbulb

densensee 伝染性 contagious

densha 電車 train (commuter train)

denshi meeru 電子メール e-mail

denshi meeru adoresu 電子メールアドレス e-mail address

denshi renji 電子レンジ microwave

dentoo 電灯 light (overhead)

dentooteki 伝統的 traditional

denwa 電話 telephone

denwa bangoo 電話番号 phone number

denwa o kakemasu 電話をかけます v dial

denwa shimasu 電話します v phone

deodoranto デオドラント deodorant

depaato デパート department store

derikatessen デリカテッセン delicatessen

dii bui dii DVD DVD

diizeru ディーゼル diesel

do 度 degrees (temperature)

dochira どちら which (polite)

doki 土器 clay pot

doko どこ where

doku 毒 poison

dokushin 独身 single (unmarried)

dono kurai どのくらい how much (quantity)

doo 銅 copper

doo itashi mashite どういたしまして you're welcome

doobutsu 動物 animal

doobutsuen 動物園 zoo

doogu 道具 equipment

dookutsu 洞窟 cave

doomo どうも hi

doomyaku 動脈 artery

...doori …通り …Street

dooro 道路 path

dooro chizu 道路地図 road map

dooryoo 同僚 colleague

dooyatte どうやって how

doozo どうぞ please (offering a favor)

doozoo 銅像 statue

dorai kuriiningu ten ドライクリーニング店 dry cleaner

dorinku menyuu ドリンクメニュー drink menu

doroboo 泥棒 thief

doru ドル dollar (U.S.)

dotchi どっち which

E

eakon エアコン air conditioning

eaponpu エアポンプ air pump

eega 映画 movie

eegakan 映画館 movie theater

eego 英語 English (language)

eegyoo jikan 営業時間 business hours

eekokujin 英国人 British

eetiiemu キャッシュコーナー ATM

eezu エイズ AIDS

eki 駅 train station/railway station [BE]

ekonomii kurasu エコノミークラス economy class

ekusukaashon エクスカーション excursion

en 円 yen

enshi 遠視 far-sighted/long-sighted [BE]

erebeetaa エレベーター elevator/lift [BE]

esukareetaa エスカレーター escalator

F

faasuto fuudo ファーストフード fast food

faasuto kurasu ファーストクラス first class

fakkusu ファックス fax

fakkusu bangoo ファックス番号 fax number

fakkusu shimasu ファックスします v fax

feesharu フェーシャル facial

ferii フェリー ferry

fiirudo フィールド field (sports)

fooku フォーク fork

fooku myuujikku フォークミュージック folk music

foomyura フォーミュラ formula (baby)

fuirumu フィルム film (camera)

fujinkai 婦人科医 gynecologist

fukaku 深く deeply

fukanabe 深鍋 pot

fukumimasu 含みます v include

fukusayoo 副作用 side effect

fukusoo kitee 服装規定 dress code

fukutsuu 腹痛 stomachache

fuminshoo 不眠症 insomnia

fun 分 minute

funsui 噴水 fountain

furaipan フライパン frying pan

furoba 風呂場 bathroom

furui 古い old (thing)

futsuka yoi 二日酔い hangover

futsuu yokin 普通預金 savings (account)

fuutoo 封筒 envelope

fuyu 冬 winter

G

gaaru furendo ガールフレンド girlfriend

gaido ガイド *n* guide

gaido bukku ガイドブック guide book

gaikokujin 外国人 foreigner

gake 崖 cliff

gakkiya 楽器屋 music store

gakkoo 学校 school

gakusee 学生 student

gamu ガム chewing gum

garasu ガラス glass (material)

gasorin ガソリン gas/petrol [BE]

gasorin sutando ガソリンスタンド gas station/petrol station [BE]

gasu ガス cooking gas

geemu ゲーム game

geeto ゲート gate (airport)

gei baa ゲイバー gay bar

gei kurabu ゲイクラブ gay club

gekijoo 劇場 theater

genkin 現金 cash

gerende ゲレンデ trail/piste [BE]

gerende chizu ゲレンデ地図 trail/piste [BE] map

geri 下痢 diarrhea

gifuto shoppu ギフトショップ gift shop

gin 銀 silver

ginkoo 銀行 bank

gochisoo sama deshita ごちそうさまでした thank you (for food)

godengon ご伝言 message

gogo 午後 afternoon/p.m.

gomen kudasai ごめんください bye

gomennasai ごめんなさい sorry

gomi ゴミ trash/rubbish [BE]

gomi bukuro ゴミ袋 garbage bag/rubbish bag [BE]

gookan 強姦 rape

gookee 合計 total (amount)

gorufu toonamento ゴルフトーナメント golf tournament

gorufujoo ゴルフ場 golf course

goshujin ご主人 husband (someone else's)

gozen 午前 a.m.

guramu グラム gram

gurasu グラス glass (drinking)

guree グレー gray

guriin グリーン green

guruupu グループ group

H

ha 歯 tooth

hagaki 葉書 postcard

haha 母 mother (one's own)

hai はい yes

hai 肺 lung

haicheaa ハイチェアー highchair

haiiro 灰色 gray

haikingu koosu annai ハイキングコース案内 trail/piste [BE] map

hairimasu 入ります *v* enter

haisha 歯医者 dentist

haiuee ハイウェー highway

hajime masu 始めます v begin

hakarimasu 測ります
  v measure (someone)

hakike 吐き気 nauseous

hakimasu 吐きます v vomit

hako 箱 box

hakubutsukan 博物館 museum

hamaki 葉巻 cigar

hamigakiko 歯磨き粉 toothpaste

han jikan 半時間 half hour

han kiro 半キロ half-kilo

hana 花 flower

hana 鼻 nose

hanashimasu 話します v speak

hanbun 半分 half

handi kyappuyoo ハンディキャップ
  用 handicapped-accessible

hando baggu ハンドバッグ
  purse/handbag [BE]

hankagai 繁華街 downtown

hanmaa ハンマー hammer

hansode 半袖 short sleeves

hanzubon 半ズボン shorts

haraimasu 払います v pay

hare 腫れ swelling

hareno 晴れの sunny

hari 鍼 acupuncture

hasami はさみ scissors

hashi 橋 bridge

hashira dokee 柱時計 wall clock

hasshin 発疹 rash

hatarakimasu 働きます v work

hatsuon shimasu 発音します
  v pronounce

hayai 早い early

hayai 速い fast

hea burashi ヘアブラシ hairbrush

hea doraiyaa ヘアドライヤー
  hair dryer

hea katto ヘアカット haircut

hea supuree ヘアスプレー hairspray

hea sutairisuto ヘアスタイリス
  ト hairstylist

hea sutairu ヘアスタイル hairstyle

heddofoon ヘッドフォーン
  headphones

heekan 閉館 closed

heeten 閉店 closed

hen 変 strange

henkoo 変更 change (plan)

hera へら spatula

herumetto ヘルメット helmet

heya 部屋 room

heya no kagi 部屋の鍵 room key

hi o tsukemasu 火をつけます
  v light (cigarette)

hi 日 day

hi 火 fire

hidari 左 left (direction)

hifu 皮膚 skin

higashi 東 east

hiitaa ヒーター heater/heating [BE]

hiji 肘 elbow

hijoo guchi 非常口 emergency exit

hikidashi 引き出し withdrawal (bank)

hikidashi masu 引き出します
  v withdraw

hikkimasu 引きます v pull

hikooki 飛行機 airplane

hikui 低い low

hima 暇 free (not busy)

hinketsu no 貧血の anemic

hiruma 昼間 noon/midday [BE]

hitchi haiku shimasu ヒッチハイクします v hitchhike

hitoban ni tsuki 一晩につき per night

hitokire 一切れ slice (of something)

hitori 一人 alone

hitotsu 一つ one

hiyake 日焼け sunburn

hiyakedome kuriimu 日焼け止めクリーム sunblock

hiyoke 日除け sunscreen

hiyoo 費用 fee

hiza 膝 knee

hizuke 日付け date (calendar)

hoka no michi 他の道 alternate route

hoken 保険 insurance

hoken gaisha 保険会社 insurance company

hoken o kakemasu 保険を掛けます v insure

hokenshoo 保険証 insurance card

hokkee ホッケー hockey

hokoosha 歩行者 pedestrian

hon 本 book

hone 骨 bone

honmono 本物 real

hon-ya 本屋 bookstore

hon-yaku shimasu 翻訳します v translate

honyuubin 哺乳瓶 baby bottle

hooki 箒 broom

hookoo 方向 direction

hoomu ホーム platform

hooseki 宝石 jewelry

hoosekiten 宝石店 jeweler

hootai 包帯 bandage

horikomimasu 彫り込みます v engrave

hoshii ndesuga 欲しいんですが I'd like…

hosuteru ホステル hostel

hoteru ホテル hotel

hozon shimasu 保存します v save (on a computer)

hyooji 表示 display

I

i 胃 stomach

ibupurofen イブプロフェン ibuprofen

ichiban ii 一番いい best

ichido 一度 once

ichiinichiikan 一日間 for (a day)

ichijikan ni tsuki 一時間につき per hour

ichijiteki 一時的 temporary

ichinichi ni tsuki 一日につき per day

idoosee 移動性 mobility

ie 家 house

igirisu イギリス United Kingdom (U.K.)

igirisujin イギリス人 English

ii 良い good
iichiketto Eチケット e-ticket
iie いいえ no
ike 池 pond
iki 行き bound
iki masu 行きます ∨ go
ikkai 一階 ground floor
ikura いくら how much (money)
ima 今 now
imooto 妹 sister (my younger)
imootosan 妹さん sister (someone else's younger)
inakunaru いなくなる missing
inryoosui 飲料水 drinking water
insatsu shimasu 印刷します ∨ print
insurin インスリン insulin
insutanto messeeji インスタント・メッセージ instant message
intaanetto インターネット internet
intaanetto kafe インターネットカフェ internet cafe
intaanetto saabisu インターネットサービス internet service
ippoo tsuukoo 一方通行 one-way street
ireba 入れ歯 denture
iremasu 入れます ∨ insert (on an ATM)
iriguchi 入口 entrance
irimasu 要ります ∨ need
iro 色 color
irui 衣類 clothing
iseki 遺跡 ruins
isha 医者 doctor

ishiki fumeino 意識不明の unconscious
ishitsubutu gakari 遺失物係 lost and found
issho 一緒 together
isshuukan ni tsuki 一週間につき per week
isu 椅子 chair
itai 痛い hurt
itami 痛み pain
itsu いつ when
itteki 一滴 drop (medicine)
iyaringu イヤリング earrings

J

jaketto ジャケット jacket
jazu ジャズ jazz
jazu kurabu ジャズクラブ jazz club
jeru ジェル gel (hair)
jidoo 自動 automatic
jidoosha toorokushoo 自動車登録証 vehicle registration
jiinzu ジーンズ jeans
jikan 時間 hour/time
jiko 事故 accident
jikokuhyoo 時刻表 timetable [BE]
jimaku 字幕 subtitle (movie)
jinja 神社 shrine
jinzoo 腎臓 kidney (body part)
jitensha 自転車 bicycle
jitensha ruuto 自転車ルート bike route
joo 錠 tablet (medicine)
jookyaku 乗客 passenger

joosha shimasu 乗車します
v board (train)

josee 女性 woman

jungin 純銀 sterling silver

junyuu shimasu 授乳します
v feed (baby)

juuden shimasu 充電します
v recharge

juusho 住所 address

K

kaado カード card

kaado de haraimasu カードで払いま
す v charge (credit card)

kaato カート cart/trolley [BE]

kaaton カートン carton

kabaa chaaji カバーチャージ
cover charge

kado no 角の on the corner

kado o magatta tokoro 角を曲がった
ところ around (the corner)

kaemasu 替えます
v exchange (money)

kaeshimasu 返します v return

kagaku 科学 science

kagi 鍵 key; lock

kagi kaado 鍵カード key card

kagi o kakemasu 鍵をかけ
ます lock up

kago かご basket (grocery store)

kai 階 floor/storey [BE]

kaichuu dentoo 懐中電灯 flashlight

kaidan 階段 stairs

kaigan 海岸 beach

kaigi 会議 meeting

kaigijoo 会議場 convention hall

kaigishitsu 会議室 meeting room

kaiin shoo 会員証 membership card

kaikan jikan 開館時間 visiting hours

kaikee 会計 n bill (of sale); cashier

kaikyoo jiin 回教寺院 mosque

kaimasu 買います v buy

kaimono 買い物 shopping

kaimono o shimasu 買い物をしま
す v shop

kajino カジノ casino

kakarimasu かかります v cost

kakekin o haraimasu 掛け金を払いま
す v place (a bet)

kaki masu 書きます v write

kakitome 書留 registered mail

kakunin shimasu 確認します
v confirm

kamera カメラ camera

kami 紙 paper

kami 髪 hair

kamisori no ha カミソリの刃
razor blade

kanada カナダ Canada

kanadajin カナダ人 Canadian

kanai 家内 wife (one's own)

kanashii 悲しい sad

kangei shimasu 歓迎します
v welcome

kangoshi 看護士 nurse

kankee 関係 relationship

kankin shimasu 換金します
v exchange (money)

kankiri 缶切り can opener

kankoo 観光 sightseeing

kankoo annaijo 観光案内所
tourist information office

kankoo tsuaa 観光ツアー
sightseeing tour

kankookyaku 観光客 tourist

kansen shita 感染した infected

kansetsu 関節 joint (body part)

kansetsuen 関節炎 arthritis

kansha shimasu 感謝します
v thank

kanyuu shimasu 加入します *v* join

kanzee 関税 duty (tax)

kanzen saabisu 完全サービス
full-service

kanzoo 肝臓 liver (body part)

kanzume 缶詰 canned

kao 顔 face

kappu カップ cup

kara ni shimasu 空にします *v* empty

karafu カラフ carafe

karai 辛い hot (spicy)

karimasu 借ります *v* rent

karorii カロリー calories

kasa 傘 umbrella

kata 肩 shoulder

katai 硬い tough (food)

katamichi 片道 one-way (ticket)

katee yoohin 家庭用品
household good

katto カット *v* cut (hair)

kawa 川 river

kawa 皮 leather

kawaii 可愛い cute

kawasereeto 為替レート
exchange rate

kaze 風邪 cold (sickness)

kazoku 家族 family

keebajoo 競馬場 racetrack

keebi 警備 security

keeburu kaa ケーブル・カー
cable car

keekiya ケーキ屋 pastry shop

keeryoo kappu 計量カップ
measuring cup

keeryoo supuun 計量スプーン
measuring spoon

keesatsu 警察 police

keesatsu no shoomeesho 警察の証
明書 police report

keesu ケース case (amount)

keetai denwa 携帯電話 cell phone/
mobile phone [BE]

kekkon shimasu 結婚します *v* marry

kekkon shiteiru 結婚している
married

kemikaru toire ケミカルトイレ
chemical toilet

kenkoo 健康 health

kenkoo shokuhinten 健康食品店
health food store

keshi masu 消します turn off (lights)

keshooshitsu 化粧室
restroom/toilet [BE]

ketsuatsu 血圧 blood pressure

ketsueki 血液 blood

ki 木 tree

kichoona 貴重な valuable

kigoo 記号 symbol (keyboard)

kigu 器具 utensil

kii horudaa キーホルダー key ring

kiiro 黄色 yellow

kikan 期間 period (of time)

kimasu 来ます v come

kin 金 gold

kin-en 禁煙 non-smoking

kinenkan 記念館 memorial (place)

kinko 金庫 safe (thing)

kinkyuu 緊急 emergent

kinniku 筋肉 muscle

kinoo 昨日 yesterday

kinshi shimasu 禁止します v prohibit

kinshi 近視 near-sighted/
short-sighted [BE]

kinu 絹 silk

kinyuu shimasu 記入します
v fill out (form)

kinyuu shite kudasai 記入してください
please fill out (form)

kiosuku キオスク newsstand

kippu 切符 ticket

kippu uriba 切符売り場 ticket office

kiree きれい clean; beautiful

kiro(guramu) キロ(グラム) kilogram

kiro(meetoru) キロ(メートル)
kilometer

kissaten 喫茶店 café/teahouse

kisu shimasu キスします v kiss

kita 北 north

kitanai 汚い dirty

kitsuenseki 喫煙席 smoking (area)

kitte 切手 n stamp (postage)

kizu 傷 n cut

kizugusuri 傷薬 antiseptic cream

kodomo 子供 child

kodomoyoo no isu 子供用の椅子
child's seat

kodomoyoo no menyuu 子供用のメニ
ュー children's menu

kodomoyoo puuru 子供用プール
kiddie pool/paddling pool [BE]

koin randorii コインランド
リー laundromat/launderette [BE]

koin rokkaa コインロッカー
luggage locker

koko ここ here

kokunai no 国内の domestic

kokunaisen 国内線 domestic flight

kokusai 国際 international
(airport area)

kokusaisen 国際線
international flight

kokuseki 国籍 nationality

kokyuu shimasu 呼吸します
v breathe

...komi ...込み with ... (included)

konban 今晩 tonight

konbanwa 今晩は good evening

konbeyaa beruto コンベヤーベル
ト conveyor belt

kondishonaa コンディショナー
conditioner

kondoomu コンドーム condom

konnichiwa 今日は hello; good
afternoon

konpyuuta コンピュータ computer

konro コンロ stove

konsaato コンサート concert

konsaato hooru コンサートホール
concert hall

konsarutanto コンサルタント consultant

konsento コンセント electric outlet

kontakuto renzu コンタクトレンズ contact lens

kontakuto renzu eki コンタクトレンズ液 contact lens solution

konzatsu 混雑 congestion

kooban 交番 police station

karai 辛い spicy

kooen 公園 *n* park/playground

kooka 硬貨 coin

kookanjo 交換所 exchange (place)

kookuu gaisha 航空会社 airline

kookuubin 航空便 airmail

kookyoo 公共 public

kooreesha 高齢者 senior citizen

koori 氷 ice

kooryoku fuyoo 抗力浮揚 drag lift

koosaten 交差点 intersection

koosee busshitsu 抗生物質 antibiotic

koosha コーシャ kosher

kooshuu denwa 公衆電話 pay phone

koosoku dooro 高速道路 highway/motorway [BE]

koosu コース route

koosui 香水 perfume

kooto コート coat

kopii コピー photocopy

koppu コップ glass (drinking)

kore これ this

koruku sukuryuu コルクスクリュー corkscrew

koshoo 故障 breakdown

kotton コットン cotton

kottooten 骨董店 antiques store

kowaremasu 壊れます *v* damage

kowareta 壊れた damaged

kozutsumi 小包 package

kubi 首 neck

kuchi 口 mouth

kuchibiru 唇 lip

kujoo 苦情 complaint

kuni bangoo 国番号 country code

kurabu クラブ club

kurai 暗い dark

kurashikku ongaku クラシック音楽 classical music

kurasu クラス class

kurejitto kaado クレジットカード credit card

kuriiningu yoohin クリーニング用品 cleaning supplies

kuroi 黒い black

kuruma 車 car

kuruma isu 車椅子 wheelchair

kuruma isu yoo suroopu 車椅子用スロープ wheelchair ramp

kuruu nekku クルーネック crew neck

kushi 櫛 comb

kusuri 薬 medicine

kutsu 靴 shoes

kutsushita 靴下 sock

kutsuya 靴屋 shoe store

kuukoo 空港 airport

kyabin キャビン cabin

kyakushitsu seesoo saabisu 客室清掃サービス housekeeping services

kyandee キャンデー candy/sweets [BE]

kyanpu kinshi キャンプ禁止 no camping

kyanpu shimasu キャンプします v camp

kyanpujoo キャンプ場 campsite

kyanseru shimasu キャンセルします v cancel

kyasshingu saabisu キャッシング・サービス cash advance

kyasshu kaado キャッシュカード ATM card

kyohi shimasu 拒否します v decline (credit card)

kyoka shimasu 許可します v permit

kyoo 今日 today

kyookai 教会 church

kyori 距離 mileage

kyuuden 宮殿 palace

kyuuka 休暇 vacation/holiday [BE]

kyuushamen 急斜面 steep

kyuukyuusha 救急車 ambulance

kyuumee booto 救命ボート life boat

kyuumee dooi 救命胴衣 life jacket

M

maaketto マーケット market

machi 町 town

machi jikan 待ち時間 n wait

machi no hiroba 町の広場 town square

machiaishitsu 待合室 waiting room

machiawasemasu 待ち合わせます v meet (someone)

machigai 間違い mistake

machimasu 待ちます v wait

mado 窓 window

madogawa 窓側 window (on flight)

madogiwa 窓際 by the window

mae 前 before

maekin 前金 deposit (security)

mago 孫 grandchild

maishuu 毎週 weekly

majimena 真面目な serious

makura 枕 pillow

manikyua マニキュア manicure

manshon マンション apartment

mantan ni shimasu 満タンにします v fill up (gasoline)

manyuaru マニュアル manual car

massaaji マッサージ massage

massugu 真っ直ぐ straight

masui 麻酔 anesthesia

maunten baiku マウンテンバイク mountain bike

mayonaka 真夜中 midnight

me 目 eye

meeru o okurimasu メールを送ります v text (send a message)

meeru shimasu メールします v e-mail

meeru メール n text (message)

meesaisho 明細書 itemized bill

meeshi 名刺 business card

megane 眼鏡 glasses

meganeten 眼鏡店 optician

memai ga shimasu めまいがします dizzy

memorii kaado メモリーカード memory card

men 綿 cotton

menyuu メニュー menu

menzee 免税 duty-free

messeeji メッセージ message

mibun shoomee 身分証明 identification

michi ni mayoi mashita 道に迷いました lost

michi 道 trail

midori 緑 green

migi 右 right (direction)

miharashidai 見晴し台 overlook (scenic place)

mihon 見本 specimen

mijikai 短い short

mimasu 見ます v see

mimasu 見ます v look

mimi 耳 ear

mimi ga kikoenai 耳が聞こえない deaf

mimi no itami 耳の痛み earache

minami 南 south

mini baa ミニバー mini-bar

minikui みにくい ugly

miryokuteki 魅力的 attractive

misa ミサ mass (church service)

misemasu 見せます v show

mizu 水 water

mizugi 水着 swimsuit

mizuumi 湖 lake

mochikomemasu 持ち込めます v allowed (on flight)

momo 腿 thigh

mondai 問題 problem

moo ichido iimasu もう一度言います v repeat

moochoo 盲腸 appendix (body part)

moodoo ken 盲導犬 guide dog

moofu 毛布 blanket

mooningu kooru モーニングコール wake-up call

mootaa booto モーターボート motor boat

mopetto モペット moped

moppu モップ mop

mori 森 forest

moshi moshi もしもし hello (on the phone)

motto もっと more

motto chiisai もっと小さい smaller

motto ii もっといい better

motto ookii もっと大きい bigger

motto ookii koe de もっと大きい声で louder

motto sukunai もっと少ない less

motto yasui もっと安い cheaper

motto yukkuri もっとゆっくり slower

muen 無鉛 unleaded (gas)

mujinno 無人の unattended

mukai 向かい opposite

mune 胸 chest (body part)
mune no itami 胸の痛み chest pain
mura 村 village
murasaki 紫 purple
muryoo 無料 free
mushi sasare 虫さされ insect bite
mushi yoke 虫除け insect repellent
mushi 虫 bug
mushiboo 無脂肪 fat free
mushiki 蒸し器 steamer
muusu ムース mousse (hair)
muzukashii 難しい difficult

N

nabe 鍋 saucepan
nagai 長い long
nagashi 流し sink
nagasode 長袖 long sleeves
naifu ナイフ knife
naisen 内線 extension (phone)
naito kurabu ナイトクラブ nightclub
nakushimasu なくします
  v lose (something)
namae 名前 name
nandemo 何でも anything
nani 何 what
nankoo 軟膏 cream (ointment)
naosemasu 直せます can fix
  (clothing)
naoshi masu 直します v alter
  (clothing)/fix
napukin ナプキン napkin
nashide 無しで without
nebukuro 寝袋 sleeping bag

nedan 値段 price/value
neeru fairu ネイルファイル nail file
neeru saron ネイルサロン nail salon
nekkuresu ネックレス necklace
nekutai ネクタイ tie (clothing)
nemuke 眠気 drowsiness
nemurimasu 眠ります v sleep
nenree 年齢 age
nenza 捻挫 sprain
netsu 熱 fever; heat
nihongo 日本語 Japanese (language)
nihonjin 日本人 Japanese (people)
nikuya 肉屋 butcher
nimotsu 荷物 luggage/baggage [BE]
nimotsu hikikae ken 荷物引換券
  luggage ticket
ningyoo 人形 doll
ninshin 妊娠 pregnant
nishi 西 west
nisshabyoo 日射病 sunstroke
nitsuki につき per
no tame ni のために for
nodo 喉 throat
nodo ga kawaki mashita 喉が渇きま
  した thirsty
nodo no itami 喉の痛み sore throat
nomikomimasu 呑み込みます
  v swallow
nomimasu 飲みます v drink; take
  (medicine)
nomimono 飲み物 drink
non arukooru ノンアルコール
  non-alcoholic
nooka 農家 farm

norikae masu 乗り換えます *v* transfer (train/flight)

norimono yoi 乗り物酔い motion sickness

nugimasu 脱ぎます take off (shoes)

nukimasu 抜きます *v* extract (tooth)

nusumaremashita 盗まれました robbed

nusumareta 盗まれた stolen

nusumimasu 盗みます *v* rob

nyuukoku tetsuzuki 入国手続き passport control

nyuuryoku shimasu 入力します *v* enter (computer)

nyuutoo futaishoo 乳糖不耐症 lactose intolerant

O

obaasan おばあさん grandmother (someone else's)

ocha お茶 tea

odorimasu 踊ります *v* dance

odoroku hodono 驚くほどの stunning

ofisu オフィス office

ofisu awaa オフィスアワー office hours

ogawa 小川 stream

ohashi おはし chopsticks

ohayoo gozaimasu お早うございます good morning

oiru オイル oil

oishii おいしい delicious

ojiisan おじいさん grand-father (someone else's)

oka 丘 hill

okaasan お母さん mother (some one else's)

okane お金 money

okanjoo お勘定 check (payment)

okoshimasu 起こします *v* wake

okugai puuru 屋外プール outdoor pool

okuremasu 遅れます *v* delay

okurimasu 送ります *v* send (mail)

okurimono 贈り物 gift

okusan 奥さん wife (someone else's)

omise kudasai お見せください *v* show (me)

omiyage お土産 souvenir

omiyageya お土産屋 souvenir store

omocha 玩具 toy

omochaya 玩具屋 toy store

omoshiroi 面白い interesting

omutsu o kaemasu おむつを替えます *v* change (baby)

omutsu おむつ diaper/nappy [BE]

onaka ga sukimashita お腹がすきました hungry

oneesan お姉さん sister (someone else's older)

onegai shimasu お願いします please (asking for a favor)

ongaku 音楽 music

onna no ko 女の子 girl

oniisan お兄さん brother (someone else's older)

onsen 温泉 hot spring; spa

oodekoron オーデコロン cologne

oofuku 往復 *n* round-trip/return [BE]

ookee オーケー OK

ookesutora オーケストラ orchestra

ookii 大きい large

oosutorariajin オーストラリア
人 Australian

ootobai オートバイ motorcycle

ootomachikku オートマチック
automatic car

opera hausu オペラハウス
opera house

opera オペラ opera

ore 俺 I (male, informal)

oremasu 折れます v break (tooth)

orenji iro オレンジ色 orange (color)

orimasu 下ります get off
(train/bus/subway)

oritatami beddo 折り畳みベッド cot

osatsu お札 bill/note [BE]

oshaburi おしゃぶり
pacifier/soother [BE]

oshiete kudasai 教えてください
v show (tell me)

oshimasu 押します v push

oshiri お尻 buttocks

oshirifuki おしりふき baby wipe

oshiro お城 castle

osoi 遅い late (time)

osoimasu 襲います v mug (attack)

osoroshii 恐ろしい terrible

osusume desu お薦めです
I recommend…

otera お寺 temple (religious)

otoko no ko 男の子 boy

otoko no hito 男の人 man

otoosan お父さん father
(someone else's)

otooto 弟 brother (my younger)

otootosan 弟さん brother
(someone else's younger)

otozuremasu 訪れます v visit

otsumami おつまみ appetizer

otsuri お釣り change (money)

otto to shibetsu shita 夫と死別し
た widowed

owarimasu 終わります v end

oyogimasu 泳ぎます v swim

oyu お湯 hot water

P

paato taimu パートタイム part-time

pajama パジャマ pajamas

pansuto パンスト
pantyhose/tights [BE]

pantii パンティー briefs (clothing)

pantsu パンツ
underwear/underpants [BE]

pan-ya パン屋 bakery

pasu waado パスワード password

pasupooto パスポート passport

pedikyua ペディキュア pedicure

peepaa taoru ペーパータオル
paper towel

pen ペン pen

penishirin ペニシリン penicillin

penisu ペニス penis

petiito ペティート petite

pikunikkujoo ピクニック場
picnic area

pinku ピンク pink

piru ピル Pill (birth control)

piza resutoran ピザ・レストラン
pizzeria

poketto ポケット pocket

pondo ポンド pound (British sterling)

pondo ポンド pound (weight)

popyuraa ongaku ポピュラー音楽 pop music

pun 分 minute

purachina プラチナ platinum

purasu saizu プラス サイズ plus size

purinto shimasu プリントします v print

puripeedo keetai プリペイド携帯 prepaid phone

puuru プール pool

R

raifu gaado ライフガード lifeguard

raitaa ライター lighter

raketto ラケット racket (sports)

randorii saabisu ランドリーサービス laundry service

rappu ラップ plastic wrap/cling film [BE]

rappu ラップ rap (music)

rasshu ラッシュ rush

ree 零 zero

reenkooto レーンコート raincoat

reesu レース lace

reeto レート exchange rate

reetooko 冷凍庫 freezer

reezooko 冷蔵庫 refrigerator

regyuraa レギュラー regular

rekkaasha レッカー車 tow truck

renraku 連絡 connection (flight)

rentakaa レンタカー rental car/hire car BE]

renzu レンズ lens

reshiito レシート receipt

ressha 列車 train

ressun レッスン lesson

resutoran レストラン restaurant

rifuto リフト lift

rifutoken リフト券 lift pass

rikon shimasu 離婚します v divorce

ringu リング ring

rinsu リンス conditioner

rippa 立派 magnificent

risaikuringu リサイクリング recycling

rittoru リットル liter

riyoo shimasu 利用します v utilize

roguofu shimasu ログオフします log off

roguon shimasu ログオンします log on

rokkaa ロッカー locker

rokkotsu 肋骨 rib (body part)

romanchikku ロマンチック romantic

roofaa ローファー loafers

rooshon ローション lotion

rosen 路線 track (train)

ruumu saabisu ルームサービス room service

ryokan 旅館 inn

ryokoo dairiten 旅行代理店 travel agency

ryokoo 旅行 trip

ryoo 寮 dormitory

ryoogae 両替 currency exchange

ryoogae shimasu 両替します
v exchange (money)

ryoogaejo 両替所 currency exchange
office

ryoojikan 領事館 consulate

ryookin meetaa 料金メーター
parking meter

ryookin 料金 charge (cost)

ryoori shimasu 料理します *v* cook

ryooshuusho 領収書 receipt

ryukkusakku リュックサック
backpack

ryuugakuseeshoo 留学生証
international student card

S

saabisu サービス service
(in a restaurant)

saafu boodo サーフボード surfboard

sabaku 砂漠 desert

saifu 財布 purse; wallet

saigo 最後 last

saikuringu サイクリング cycling

sainshimasu サインします *v* sign

saisho no 最初の first

saizu サイズ size

sakana 魚 fish

sakaya 酒屋 liquor store/off-licence
[BE]

sakkaa サッカー soccer

sakkaa geemu サッカーゲーム
soccer/football [BE] game

sakujo shimasu 削除します
v delete

samui 寒い cold (weather)

sandaru サンダル sandals

sangurasu サングラス
sunglasses

sanpo 散歩 *n* walk

sanpomichi 散歩道 walking route

sanshoo 山頂 peak (of a mountain)

sanso chiryoo 酸素治療
oxygen treatment

sara araiki 皿洗い機 dishwasher

sara 皿 plate

sauna サウナ sauna

sayoonara さようなら goodbye

seebyoo 性病 sexually transmitted
disease (STD)

seekyuu shimasu 請求します
v bill (charge)

seekyuusho 請求書 invoice

seeri 生理 period (menstrual)

seeriyoo napukin 生理用ナプキ
ン sanitary napkin/pad [BE]

seetaa セーター sweater

seiritsuu 生理痛 menstrual cramp

seki 咳 cough

seki 席 seat

sekitsui 脊椎 spine (body part)

sekken 石鹸 soap

seminaa セミナー seminar

sen 線 line (train)

senaka 背中 back (body part)

senchi meetoru センチメートル
centimeter

senjooato 戦場跡 battleground

senjoozai 洗浄剤 cleaning product

senmon-i 専門医 specialist (doctor)

senmonka 専門家 expert (skill level)

sennuki 栓抜き bottle opener

senpuuki 扇風機 fan (appliance)

sensui yoogu 潜水用具 diving equipment

sentaku 洗濯 laundry

sentaku shisetsu 洗濯施設 laundry facility

sentakuki 洗濯機 washing machine

senzai 洗剤 detergent

serufu saabisu セルフサービス self-service

sesshi 接氏 Celsius

setomono 瀬戸物 china

setsuzoku 接続 connection (internet)

setsuzoku o kirimasu 接続を切ります disconnect (computer)

setsuzoku shimasu 接続します v connect (internet)

shanpuu シャンプー shampoo

shashin 写真 photo

shashin satsuee 写真撮影 photography

shatsu シャツ shirt

shawaa シャワー shower

sheebingu kuriimu シェービングクリーム shaving cream

shiai 試合 n match

shibai 芝居 n play (theater)

shichakushitsu 試着室 fitting room

shigai chizu 市街地図 town map

shigai kyokuban 市外局番 area code

shigoto 仕事 business

shihainin 支配人 manager (restaurant, hotel)

shihee 紙幣 n bill (money)/note [BE]

shii dii CD CD

shiitsu シーツ sheet

shikaku shoogaisha 視覚障害者 visually impaired

shikki 漆器 lacquerware

shimasu します v play

shimemasu 閉めます v close (a shop)

shinbun 新聞 newspaper

shindai 寝台 berth

shindaisha 寝台車 sleeper car

shingoo 信号 traffic light

shinguru beddo シングルベッド single bed

shinguru ruumu シングルルーム single room

shinju 真珠 pearl

shinnyuu shimasu 侵入します break-in (burglary)

shintai shoogaisha 身体障害者 disabled; handicapped

shinzoo 心臓 heart

shinzoobyoo 心臓病 heart condition

shirabemasu 調べます v check (something)

shirasemasu 知らせます v notify

shiroi 白い white

shisnkoku shimasu 申告します v declare

shita 舌 tongue

shitagi 下着 underwear

shitsu 質 quality

shitsumon 質問 question

shitsunai puuru 室内プール
indoor pool

shitsuree shimasu 失礼します
excuse me (to get past)

shiyakusho 市役所 town hall

shizen hogoku 自然保護区
nature preserve

shizuka 静か quiet

shohoo shimasu 処方します
v prescribe

shohoosen 処方箋 prescription

shohoosen nashi 処方箋無し
over the counter (medication)

shokki 食器 dish (kitchen)

shokubutsuen 植物園
botanical garden

shokudoo 食堂 dining room

shokuji 食事 meal

shokuryoohin 食料品 produce

shokuryoohinten 食料品店
grocery store

shomeeshimasu 署名します v sign

shooboosho 消防署 fire department

shoogo 正午 noon

shoohizee 消費税 sales tax

shoojoo 症状 condition (medical)

shookai shimasu 紹介します
v introduce

shookeesu ショーケース
display case

shookyo shimasu 消去します
v clear (on an ATM)

shoonikai 小児科医 pediatrician

shooten gai 商店街 shopping area

shoppingu mooru ショッピングモー
ル shopping mall

shoshinsha 初心者 novice (skill level)

shujin 主人 husband(one's own)

shukketsu shimasu 出血します
v bleed

shukuboo 宿坊 temple
accommodation

shukuhaku setsubi 宿泊設備
accommodation

shuppatsu 出発 departure

shusseki shimasu 出席します
v attend

shuu 週 week

shuuji yoogu 習字用具
calligraphy supplies

shuumatsu 週末 weekend

shuuri shimasu 修理します v repair

shuurikoo 修理工 mechanic

shuurikoojoo 修理工場 garage

sobo 祖母 grandmather (one's own)

sofu 祖父 grandfather (one's own)

sofubo 祖父母 grandparents
(one's own)

soko そこ there

sokutatsu 速達 express

sookin shimasu 送金します
v transfer (money)

soonyuu shimasu 挿入します
v insert (on an ATM)

soto 外 outside

...sugimasu …過ぎます too…

sugoi すごい amazing

suihanki 炊飯器 rice cooker

suijoo sukii 水上スキー water skis

suisen shimasu 推薦します
v recommend

suisen 推薦 recommendation

suishoo 水晶 crystal

sukaafu スカーフ scarf

sukaato スカート skirt

sukidesu 好きです *v* like

sukii スキー ski

sukii rifuto スキーリフト chair lift

sukoshi 少し little

sukyanaa スキャナー scanner

sumi 炭 charcoal

sumimasen すみません
excuse me (apology)

sumimasu 住みます *v* live

sunakku baa スナックバー snack bar

suniikaa スニーカー sneaker

sunoo boodo スノーボード
snowboard

sunookeru yoogu スノーケル用
具 snorkeling equipment

supiido ihan スピード違反 speeding

supootsu スポーツ sports

supootsu yoohinten スポーツ用品
店 sporting goods store

supuun スプーン spoon

suriipingu baggu スリーピングバッグ
sleeping bag

surippa スリッパ slippers

surudoi 鋭い sharp

sushi ya 寿司屋 sushi restaurant

sutaato shimasu スタートします
v start (a car)

sutajiamu スタジアム stadium

suteki すてき nice

sutokku ストック poles (skiing)

suuji 数字 number

suupaa スーパー super (fuel)

suupaa スーパー supermarket

suutsu スーツ suit

suutsu keesu スーツケース
suitcase

suwarimasu 座ります *v* sit

suzushii 涼しい cool (temperature)

T

taaminaru ターミナル
terminal (airport)

tabako 煙草 cigarette

tabako o suimasu 煙草を吸います
v smoke

tabakoya 煙草屋 tobacconist

tabeamasu 食べます *v* eat

tabemono 食物 food

tachiiri kinshi 立入禁止 no access

tada ただ only

taika tobira 耐火扉 fire door

taipu shimasu タイプします *v* type

taishoku shita 退職した retired

taiya タイヤ tire/tyre [BE]

taiyoo 太陽 sun

takai 高い expensive; high

taki 滝 waterfall

takibi kinshi 焚火禁止 no fires

takushii タクシー taxi

tanima 谷間 valley

tanjoobi 誕生日 birthday

tanoshii 楽しい happy

tanoshimi 楽しみ pleasure

tanoshimimasu 楽しみます
v enjoy

tanpon タンポン tampon

taoru タオル towel

tasuke 助け help

tasukete 助けて help me!

tatemono 建物 building

te 手 hand

teeburu テーブル table

omochikaeri お持ち帰り
take-out/take away [BE]

tegami 手紙 letter/post [BE]

tekubi 手首 wrist

tenchoo 店長 manager (shop)

tenimotsu 手荷物 carry-on/hand
luggage [BE]

tenimotsu hikikaeshoo 手荷物引換
証 baggage ticket

tenimotsu hikiwatashijo 手荷物引渡
所 baggage claim

tenisu テニス tennis

tenki 天気 weather

tennai no annai 店内の案内
store directory

tento テント tent

tento no shichuu テントの支柱
tent pole

tento yoo pegu テント用ペグ
tent peg

terakotta テラコッタ terracotta

terebi テレビ TV

terehon kaado テレホンカード
phone card

tii shatsu Tシャツ T-shirt

tisshu peepaa ティッシュペーパー
tissue

tobikomimasu 飛び込みます v dive

todokimasu 届きます v reach

toire トイレ bathroom (toilet)

toire no kyuuingu トイレの吸引
具 plunger

toiretto peepaa トイレットペーパ
ー toilet paper

tokoya 床屋 barber

tokubetsuna 特別な extra

tokudai 特大 extra large

tomarimasu 止まります v stop

tomarimasu 泊まります
v stay (overnight)

too 塔 tower

toochaku 到着 arrivals (airport)

tooi 遠い far

toojoo ken 搭乗券 boarding pass

toojoo shimasu 搭乗します
v board (plane)

tooki 陶器 pottery

toonan 盗難 theft

toonyoobyoo 糖尿病 diabetic

tooza yokin 当座預金 checking
accoun/current account [BE]

tooza yoking kooza 当座預金口
座 checking account

toraberaazu chekku トラベラーズチ
ェック traveler's check/traveller's
cheque [BE]

toreenaa トレーナー sweatshirt

toreeningu jimu トレーニングジム
gym

tori 鳥 bird

torikaemasu 取り替えます
  v exchange (goods)

torimu トリム trim (hair cut)

toshi 年 year

toshiyori 年寄り old (person)

toshokan 図書館 library

tsuaa ツアー tour

tsugi 次 next

tsukaemasen 使えません
  doesn't work

tsukaimasu 使います *v* use

tsukaisute 使い捨て disposable

tsukaisute kamisori 使い捨てカミソ
  リ disposable razor

tsukare mashita 疲れました tired

tsukareta 疲れた exhausted

tsukemasu つけます turn on (lights)

tsukeawase 付け合わせ side dish

tsukimasu 着きます *v* arrive

tsuki 月 month

tsuki 付き with... (attached)

tsumaranai つまらない boring

tsume 爪 fingernail

tsumemasu 詰めます *v* pack

tsumemono 詰物 filling (tooth)

tsumetai 冷たい cold (food)

tsuretekimasu 連れてきます *v* bring

tsutsumimasu 包みます
  v wrap (a package)

tsuuka 通貨 currency

tsuuro 通路 aisle

tsuurogawa no zaseki 通路側の座
  席 aisle seat

tsuuyakusha 通訳者 interpreter

tsuzuri o iimasu つづりを言います
  v spell

U

ubaguruma 乳母車 stroller

ude dokee 腕時計 watch

ude 腕 arm

ueetaa ウェーター waiter

ueetoresu ウェートレス waitress

ueno 上の upper

uketorimasu 受け取ります
  v pick up (something)

uketsuke 受付 reception

umi 海 sea

unten menkyoshoo 運転免許証
  driver's license

unten menkyoshoo bangoo 運転免許
  証番号 driver's license number

unten shimasu 運転します *v* drive

urimasu 売ります *v* sell

urin 雨林 rainforest

ushiro 後ろ behind (direction)

utsukushii 美しい beautiful

uuru ウール wool

W

waiaresu intaanetto ワイアレスイン
  ターネット wireless internet

waiaresu intaanetto saabisu ワイア
  レスインターネットサービス wireless
  internet service

wain risuto ワインリスト wine list

wakai 若い young

wakarimasen 分かりません
I don't understand

wakarimasu 分かります
v understand

wanpiisu ワンピース dress
(piece of clothing)

waribiki 割引 discount

watakushi 私 I (formal)

Y

yakemasu 焼けます *v* burn

yakisugi 焼き過ぎ overdone

yakkyoku 薬局 pharmacy/chemist [BE]

yakyuu 野球 baseball

yama 山 mountain

yasashii やさしい easy

yasui 安い inexpensive

yatoimasu 雇います *v* rent/hire [BE]

yoboo sesshu 予防接種 vaccination

yodooshi 夜通し overnight

yohoo 予報 forecast

yoku yasumi mashita よく休みまし
た well-rested

yoofukuya 洋服屋 clothing store

yooi ga dekite iru 用意ができてい
る ready

yooshi 用紙 form (fill-in)

yoru 夜 night

yotee 予定 *n* schedule

yotee ni iremasu 予定に入れます *v*
schedule

yoyaku madoguchi 予約窓口
reservation desk

yoyaku shimasu 予約します
v reserve

yoyaku 予約 appointment;
reservation

yubi 指 finger

yubiwa 指輪 ring

yuki no ooi 雪の多い snowy

yukigutsu 雪靴 snowshoe

yukkuri ゆっくり slowly

yurushimasu 許します *v* excuse

yuubin posuto 郵便ポスト
mailbox/postbox [BE]

yuubinkyoku 郵便局 post office

yuuenchi 遊園地 amusement park

yuugata 夕方 evening

yuujin 友人 friend

yuukoo 有効 valid

yuusenken 優先権 right of way

yuusoo shimasu 郵送します
v mail

yuusu hosuteru ユースホステル
youth hostel

yuuzaa mee ユーザー名
username

Z

zasshi 雑誌 magazine

zeekan 税関 customs

zeekan shinkokusho 税関申告書
customs declaration form

zensai 前菜 appetizer/starter [BE]

zensoku no 喘息の asthmatic

zero ゼロ zero

zubon ズボン pants/trousers [BE]

zutsuu 頭痛 headache

zutsuuyaku 頭痛薬 aspirin

Amanpuri, Thailand

JOIN THE CLUB!

Earn Rewards, Get Discounts, Stay Free, Only with HotelClub! Across 30,000 Hotels in 120 Countries

£10 OFF
see reverse for details

...with discounts and free
...ery booking made by you
...Member Dollars.

...Account with **£10* Member Dollars** – which you can ...**Club.com** booking. Log on to **www.HotelClub.com/berlitzphrase** to activate your **HotelClub.com** Membership. Complete your details, including the Membership Number & Password located on the back of the **HotelClub.com** card.

Over 4.5 million Members already use Member Dollars to pay for all or part of their hotel bookings. Join now and start spending Member Dollars whenever and wherever you want – you are not restricted to specific hotels or dates!

With great savings of up to 60% on over 30,000 hotels across 120 countries, you are sure to find the perfect location for business or pleasure. Happy travels from **HotelClub.com!**

* Equivalent to USD $17. One Member Dollar – USD $1

www.berlitzpublishing.com

Amanpuri, Thailand

**HotelClub.com
Membership
Discount Card**

Register with

HotelClub.com

**and
get £10!**

At *HotelClub.com*, we reward our Members with discounts and free
stays in their favourite hotels. As a Member, every booking made by you
through *HotelClub.com* will earn you Member Dollars.

When you register, we will credit your Member Account with *£10* Member
Dollars* - which you can use on your next *HotelClub.com* booking. Log on to
www.HotelClub.com/berlitzphrase to activate your *HotelClub.com* Membership.
Complete your details, including the Membership Number & Password
located on the back of the *HotelClub.com* card.

Over 4.5 million Members already use Member Dollars to pay for all or part of
their hotel bookings. Join now and start spending Member Dollars whenever and
wherever you want - you are not restricted to specific hotels or dates!

With great savings of up to 60% on over 30,000 hotels across 120 countries,
you are sure to find the perfect location for business or pleasure.
Happy travels from *HotelClub.com!*

www.berlitzpublishing.com

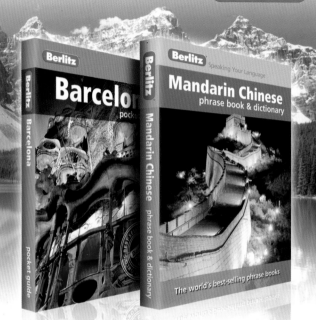

Discover the World, Speak the Language

With more than 40 million copies sold worldwide,
Berlitz Pocket Guides are renowned for their trustworthy
coverage and remarkable portability. And, if you're ever stuck
for words, the equally portable Berlitz Phrase Books have the
answers in 30 languages, from Arabic to Swahili.